MW00879590

# TALES OF A COUNTRY SHOWGIRL

## Jan Sherman

Copyright 2020 by Jan Sherman
Published by Jan North Productions

**ISBN:** 9798566637853

All rights reserved. No part of this book may be reproduced or transmitted in any form or by any means electronic or mechanical, including photocopying, recording, or by any information storage and retrieval system without written permission from the author, except for the inclusion of brief quotations in a review.

Editor: June Gossler Anderson

Cover Design: Dan Sherman

Interior Layout and Design: Todd Anderson

**Acknowledgements**

Thank you to my grandsons, Dan & Jon Sherman, for their encouragement, guidance, and continued support with this book. Also, to all my grandchildren who have asked why I never talk about my music career. Hope you enjoy this my darlings, I love you to the moon and back!

**Dedication**

This book is dedicated to my three wonderful sons! You have been my pride and joy since you were born. How blessed I am to be your mother!

*Jonny, Jody & Jeff Sherman*

# Growing Up Years – (1943-1953)

*Tales of a Country Showgirl*

## My Inspiration

My love for music stemmed from watching my father, Harley Northrop, play his guitar and sing old cowboy songs. Listening to him was one of my earliest memories and I was quite fascinated by his music. I loved to sit on the floor and just listen to him sing. One of the saddest songs was called "Little Joe the Wrangler."

As I got a little older, I wanted to learn how to play the guitar, too. My father taught me some very simple chords that I could play just using one string--one string for a C and one string for a G7. I learned how to play an open chord and even though my fingers really hurt, I kept on playing. I remember strumming with my thumb and trying to sing some of those old cowboy songs. After a while, I had such a huge blister on my thumb that I couldn't strum anymore. So, I got a matchbook cover and I folded it up and used that for a guitar pick. My dad always strummed with his thumb or with his fingernails, never a guitar pick. We had a lot of fun with that guitar!

I was five years old in 1943 when our family moved to Duluth, Minnesota. My father had gotten a job in that city installing floor coverings. So, my parents packed up a four-wheel trailer with all of our belongings along with their three children. My sister Pat was the oldest, I was fourteen months younger, and a couple years younger than me was my brother Butch.

As we were driving into Duluth and going up a little bit of a grade, a drunk driver came barreling down the hill and hit us head on! The four-wheel trailer rolled over and down a huge embankment. My brother, Butch, went through the windshield. He was badly hurt. Pat was sitting in the middle of the front seat. The top of the shift knob flew off and the shifter stick punctured her ankle and went all the way up to her knee. Later at the hospital the doctor wanted to amputate her leg, but my father wouldn't hear of it. He picked her up and left and found a new doctor who helped her heal. I had a few facial cuts. The doctors put a big clamp on my eyelid where it was cut. Pat and Butch were in the hospital for a long time. I know my parents were injured a lot worse than they let anybody know. One of the saddest memories, of course, was that my father's guitar got wrecked right along with everything else we owned. It was a terribly bad accident. We all had a lot of healing to do.

We made it to Duluth where we lived on a big farm. It was beautiful and peaceful with lots of baby chicks for company. With no guitar, there wasn't much music in the house. Eventually, Dad got another guitar and taught me a few more chords. I got out my matchbook cover and folded it all up for my pick and started singing.

After a couple of years in Duluth, we moved to Stillwater to care for one of my dad's uncles. I was now in the second grade. I had a red cowboy hat and all I needed was a pair of red cowboy boots to match. My parents made a huge sacrifice for my birthday that year and bought me a pair of red cowboy boots. They were my prized possessions.

I told my teacher that I could play a guitar and sing, so she invited me to come and play for the class. My sister, Pat, carried my red cowboy hat so I could carry my guitar on my head since we didn't have a guitar case. After walking about six or seven blocks to school, I played for my class, singing all the cowboy songs that I knew. Then my teacher asked if I would go into the other classrooms and sing for some of the children there as well. I loved it. I was not bashful at all and I ended up singing for everybody at the school. I had a song in my heart. I also had blisters on my feet from walking that far in my red cowboy boots!

**From the Garage to the Big Stage**

Later during my childhood, my family moved to a farmhouse on Little Canada Road in Little Canada, MN. The landscape was very different back then in the Forties. We had a large barn and a two and a half car garage, along with some outbuildings. We raised chickens and would collect and sell their eggs. We even had a little baby pig, which grew up to be a huge pig!

I was really interested in music. I loved to sing, dance and play my guitar. My sister, Penny, and I took dance lessons for a while, but she didn't like it and quit. I loved to dance and decided to continue without Penny. I had a recording of "Chattanooga

5

Shoeshine Boy," and my dance instructor worked out a dance for me to perform to that song. I had my little tap dance shoes, a cute little red suit, and a red hat. My dad made me a shoeshine box with a big leather strap. I would hang sheets up in the garage for a stage curtain and set up a whole bunch of chairs and benches. I charged everybody a dime to get in to see my shows. I would play my guitar and sing the cowboy songs I knew. I also performed my tap-dancing number. Over the years I have run into quite a few people who still remember the shows that I put on as a child in Little Canada. I was passionate about music and loved being on a stage in front of people. It was great fun, and I really enjoyed performing. It even put a little jingle in my pocket.

My parents had some close friends who owned a club on 14th and Robert Street in St. Paul. I remember my father taking me there. This was around the time I was doing my garage shows in Little Canada. I would sit on the end of the bar, playing the guitar and singing for a couple hours each Saturday afternoon. Sometimes, my mother would come, and she and I would polka. I used to love dancing with my mother. I was so happy that the customers enjoyed my singing, even though my repertoire was not so great at that time.

## My Love Affair with the Accordion

When I was twelve, I got rheumatic fever and was very sick. I was hospitalized and developed a heart murmur. I couldn't do anything. I couldn't play outside, couldn't ski, couldn't ice skate, couldn't do anything that my sisters and brothers were doing because of the heart murmur. I was pretty much bedridden, so I watched a lot of TV. The only good part was that the nurses would come and bring me malts whenever I wanted because I was so underweight.

I could have vanilla, chocolate, or strawberry. I thought, "This is unbelievable! I'm in hog heaven!" I had three malts a day and could have had even more than that if I had wanted. After the first few days I was getting a little tired of the malts, so I'd give them to my relatives when they came to visit. After a while I would hold them in my hands to try to melt them and spill them so the nurses would think it was an accident. Even though I wasn't supposed to get out of bed, I had to get rid of those terrible malts so I would go into the bathroom and flush them down the toilet. When my friends came to visit, I'd give them a malt. They loved them. After my hospital stay, I couldn't stand the sight of a malt, much less the smell of one. I was nauseated by malts for the next forty years of my life.

One day during the time that I was bedridden with rheumatic fever, I was watching TV and all of a sudden I saw a handsome man playing an instrument. I absolutely fell in love with the music and with the instrument as well, even though I had no idea what it was called. My father told me it was an accordion and I learned that the guy playing it was Dick Contino. He was a flashy Italian who wore a shirt with big billowing sleeves as he played "Lady of Spain." Dick Contina was quite a showman. In fact, he was marvelous! I told my father I wanted to learn how to play that instrument so my mother called the doctor to see if he thought it would hurt me because of the heart murmur. I was rather despondent at that time because I couldn't do anything except lay in my bed or sit in a chair. I lived like an invalid and I hated it. The doctor said they would have to monitor my heart because he didn't want me to do any more damage to it. My parents let me start taking accordion lessons. I was so happy!

I met Dick Contino several years later when he was appearing at Mancini's in St. Paul. We shared a pot of coffee and I told him it was all his fault that I ended up in the music

*Jan, Dick Contino & Johnny Konchal*

industry. I told him my story about seeing him on TV, and the impact it had on me. If I hadn't seen him on TV playing an instrument that I couldn't identify, it's possible I would never have played an accordion and gone on to be a professional musician.

## Learning to Play the Heaviest Instrument of All Time

I started taking lessons at Torps Music Center, playing a little twelve base accordion. I absolutely loved it! I would go through two books a week that my instructor gave me. All I wanted to do was sit and play the accordion.

My parents decided they should learn to play the instrument as well. My mother would do the right hand; my dad would learn the left hand. That lasted about three days because between the two of them, they just couldn't grasp it.

On my third or fourth week of lessons, Mr. Torp asked me if I would play on TV. My instructor, Johnny Konchal, had written a very wonderful rendition of "Lady of Spain" just for me. I practiced and practiced and practiced for my appearance on one of the local TV stations. My mother had bought me an outfit for the occasion with big billowing sleeves, just like Dick Contino wore. I wanted to be a showman like him. I went on TV and played "Lady of Spain" with all the pizzazz I could muster. That included some very intricate fingering with the arrangement that my instructor had written for me and the "bellows shake," which was a challenge. I had struggled with that but not on the day of the TV show. I enjoyed the experience of being on that TV show a lot.

I took lessons from Johnny Konchal until he stopped teaching, then I continued my lessons with Eddie Lewandowski. Eddie was an absolute genius on an accordion. His wife, Nancy, was also a very good jazz musician in the Twin Cities.

## Name Change

My parents named me JoAnn. In school, most of my friends called me Jo. When I started singing, I didn't think Jo was a very feminine name, so I decided to change it. I sat down with my parents to ask what they thought. My father came up with the funny name "Johan, Josephy, Frangesco, Antonio, Armando Nicopopolis!" My mother's favorite name for me was "The Black-Eyed Devil." Oh, brother!

My sister, Pat, was fourteen months older than me and couldn't pronounce my name, so she started calling me Jan, which was the initials of my name, <u>J</u>o <u>A</u>nn <u>N</u>orthrop, and we all thought that name worked quite well. Because my last name was Northrop, we decided to go with North. Short and easy to remember! So, Jan North it was!

# On The Road - (1953-1956)

## The Irene Brown Trio - My First Gig

One day Mr. Torp called my mother and said there was a woman looking for an accordion player to play some jobs with her and asked if I would be interested. Her name was Irene Brown. She came to our house and I did a bit of an audition for her. She said she had other people she was going to audition as well. At the time, I had agreed to volunteer my time with a variety group of entertainers: dancers and horn players, vocalists, and even a magician! I was to play my accordion. Of course, I played my signature number, "Lady of Spain," along with many other popular songs as well. Our group of entertainers would be taken on a bus to visit some hospitals and perform for the patients. A couple of times we went into prisons and played for the inmates. I enjoyed traveling around and getting to know all these people that played different instruments and to entertain people in different venues. I was a soloist at that time and just played my accordion. I didn't sing, I just played instrumental music. None of us were paid to perform but our audiences sure enjoyed all the entertainment. It was a great experience.

When I was first asked to play with the Irene Brown Trio, I wasn't quite sure if it was the right choice for me. At the time, I was only 15 years old. My parents were having a difficult time making a decision to allow me to quit school to pursue my musical career. They confided in my grandparents and asked them what they thought about it. They all agreed to let me try it and see how it worked out. This was the beginning of it all. I had a song in my heart and a whole bunch of ambition!

After my audition I was invited to join the Irene Brown Trio and play music with them on the road. The trio was made up of Irene Brown, her sister Lue Brown, and myself. Irene was a redheaded steel guitar player, but she only played a couple songs. She also played the drums. Lue was blonde, sang well, and played rhythm guitar. I was at a disadvantage since I didn't know any of their material and they didn't have any music. Well, I knew this was going to be an experience! I got together with Lue and ran over some of the songs that she sang but I had no sheet music to follow. I had never played or backed a singer before, so it was a difficult experience. Nevertheless, we started rehearsing together and before we knew it, we had a job booked in Austin, Minnesota even though I still didn't know much of their material at that time. I played a lot of solo accordion but didn't do much singing at that time. I was still in high school!

When the gig came up, we headed down to the club in Austin. The first day there the sisters decided I needed lots of makeup. My freckles needed to be covered up. They had something called "pancake makeup" to do the job. I had never heard of it before. It was like mixed-up cement! As they put it on my face, I realized that I had better be smiling because my face would be stuck in that expression for the rest of the night. The pancake make-up was applied with a wet sponge along with tons and tons of eye make-up and tons and tons of lipstick! I had never worn makeup in my life and all of a sudden there I was with all of this stuff plastered on my face! At that point I was questioning myself as to whether or not I wanted to be a musician. Yikes! What did I get myself into?

Since I was underage, the sisters came up with a plan. If anyone asked, I would tell them that I was recently divorced and I wasn't interested in meeting any man. I pretty much stayed to myself. I thought it was a totally bizarre story, but that's what they went with and told anybody that would listen. When, in fact, I was 15 years old and probably had one date in my entire life! I was totally petrified working in that club. My father and my mother would come to Austin on the weekends and watch me perform on Saturday nights. They often brought my grandmother and a couple of my aunts as well.. One of my aunts had some ideas about what I should do with my hair because I'm sure I looked like I was 15.

At first, I was sick to my stomach because I was so nervous about this job. I was so out of my element that I threw up for the first three nights. Not fun. I just wanted to go back home and be with my family and I missed school. I had been a good student. I was valedictorian of my eighth-grade class and had had fantastic grades when I was in high school. I turned 16 shortly after leaving that job in Austin. I could leave school with no trouble, I was torn. I should have stayed in school, but I so wanted to be a singer and entertainer.

When I got back in town, I joined the musician's union. Although I wasn't supposed to, the union let me play for those few weeks. Irene went to the union (Local 30 in St. Paul) and told them that her keyboard player had left and she had found someone to fill in. She asked if the union could give me a pass to play in Austin for the three weeks, and then I would come and join the union afterwards. I went to the union hall to join the local. I didn't have to do any auditioning for them because I had already played professionally with Irene and she had been a member of the union for a long time. They encouraged me to go to the union meetings to learn a few things.

The first union meeting I went to was on 9th and Wabasha, up above Alary's Bar. Ella Fitzgerald was in town with her keyboard player at the time, so she came to the union meeting and performed for us. It was so marvelous. She was gracious and wonderful to everybody. It was amazing to meet Ella Fitzgerald. Even though I was familiar with some of her songs, I wasn't especially familiar with her. But, after meeting her and seeing her perform, I certainly did become a big fan of hers.

The Irene Brown trio continued to work at a couple of clubs around town. We were working in Minneapolis for a while and we booked a two-week contract with options, meaning if they didn't like us after two weeks they could give us notice or if we didn't care for the club we could give them notice and move on. Some of these clubs we stayed at for months. The Midway Gardens was a big club on University Avenue that had live music six nights a week. Mondays, Tuesdays, and Wednesdays I would work with the Irene Brown Trio and on Thursdays, Fridays, and Saturdays I was a vocalist with the George Bordaneau Quartet. The members of the quartet played various instruments and they played them very well. The club had a big dance floor and served food. It was a very nice establishment. When I sang with the quartet, I would sit on a chair; then come to the mike and sing one or two numbers for each set.. Then, I would sit back down. I didn't have to work very hard!

As time went on, Irene and Lue started getting into arguments more and more often. After one of these arguments, Lue was so upset she left the group. Irene hired another girl who played bass to take her place. Lue's replacement didn't play particularly well, but she sang good enough. She played music with us for a couple of weeks at the Midway Club and I continued to sing Thursday, Friday, and Saturday with the men's quartet.

One night as I was singing with the quartet, the owner asked me to come in the office and speak with him. When I got to his office, he introduced me to two detectives from the St. Paul morals squad who wanted to see my identification. At that time, I was only 16 years old. I didn't have identification, so I apologized and told them I would talk to my parents and see if they could bring it down. They told me not to worry about it tonight. They would come back the following evening and check with me again. After they left, I confessed to the owner of the club that I was only 16 years old and I didn't want to cause any problems for him. He was flabbergasted. That meant that our all-girl band couldn't perform anymore because they didn't have anyone to play a lead instrument. Even though Irene played steel guitar, she only played maybe a half a dozen numbers and the other girl played bass, but not very well. I was their only lead player.

I left the club that night after the morals squad had come in. I walked down the street, went to a phone booth, and called my mother. She came down to pick me up since my father was deer hunting at the time. I was glad to get out of there and not have any more problems. So, when the police came back the next day, the owner told them that I was no longer playing music there.

*Jan North and Irene Brown*

## The Charmettes--Lue and I Team up

A week later, I got a call from Lue, who wanted to try and find some work together for us as a duo. I figured that would be better than nothing because I had already quit school and I wanted to continue to work. We made good money because we were in the union and were paid union wages.

We met with a man in Minneapolis named Joe Billo. He was a booking agent with a company called Consolidated Artists, who had one office in Minneapolis and one office in Milwaukee, Wisconsin. We talked to him and he said he could get us booked as a duo if we had some professional pictures taken and we paid a percentage of our wages to the company. We decided to give it a try. So, we went and had some professional pictures taken of us and coined the name "The Charmettes." Joe sent the pictures to a couple different clubs. He called us back in a week and said he had found some work for us on the road; that he could book us at multiple clubs, where we would stay for two weeks and then move on to a new one further south. He said we could work down the east coast, all the way to Miami, Florida! Wow, I was over the moon!

Our first gig as The Charmettes was at the Black Bear Lounge in Chisholm, Minnesota. At that time, the iron mines in northern Minnesota were a very popular place to work. It was a wealthy community up there, so the residents had a lot of money to spend on entertaining themselves. When we got there, we saw ads all over the town for our upcoming performance at the Black Bear Lounge. The big ads also said that we were "Direct from Las Vegas." I had never been out of the State of Minnesota. I remember hoping that nobody asked questions about Las Vegas, because I would have had a look on my face that resembled a jackass eating thistles!

Our next job was at a club in the upper peninsula of Michigan. The club was beautiful. I was impressed by the sizzling steaks served on platters. There again, we were billed as "Direct from Las Vegas." Attached to the club was a small apartment for the entertainers to stay in. Lue and I shared the apartment. We each had our own bedrooms with a small kitchenette where we could make ourselves something to eat if we wanted.

One Sunday night, Lue decided to go out to eat with a gentleman that she had met at the club. I told her to go have a good time, I had all my movie magazines to read and that's all I needed. My mother had bought me a beautiful lounging outfit. It was a white satin jacket that had a tie belt around the waist and comfortable black satin pants. I took a shower, relaxed, and lounged in the apartment by myself that Sunday evening until I heard a knock at the door. It was the owner of the club, who told me that I had a phone call and I should go to the kitchen area to take it. I was so upset, my heart sank because I thought something was wrong with my parents or my siblings back at home.

I ran to a small phone booth where you had to talk to the operator. I picked up the phone, told the operator that my name was Jan North and I had a phone call come into this club. She told me there was no phone call for me. All of a sudden I looked up and the owner of the club was holding his arms on both sides of the phone booth, blocking me in. I couldn't get out! I was petrified! I hung the phone up and I shot right through, underneath his arm, and got out of the phone booth. But I couldn't escape. He had locked the doors to the place and was chasing me! He grabbed me, and then tried to assault me, tearing the sleeve and belt out of my quilted white satin jacket. He was grabbing me, putting his mouth on my neck and I was screaming bloody murder but there was no one to hear me! It was Sunday and not a soul was in that place. My assailant was tall and much stronger than I was. He kept grabbing me and trying to bend me backward on the worktable in the back area. I got away and ran to the door but the door was locked. I grabbed a knife off of one of the counters and told him if he didn't let me out of the building, I would stab him. Once I swung the knife at him, he started to settle down and even tried to apologize. I backed up to let him unlock the door. I didn't trust him and told him to stand away on the other side of the room while I got out of there. I dropped the knife and ran out the door through a little alcove into my apartment and locked the door. I was so upset. I couldn't stop shaking and I couldn't stop crying. I figured since he owned the club, he probably had a key to the apartment that I was staying in. I couldn't believe how upset I was. I couldn't call my parents and I couldn't call the police. I didn't know what I could do because I was only 16 years old and I wasn't supposed to be performing in the first place. I had signed a contract and we had jobs booked all the way down to Savannah, Georgia.

I cried myself to sleep every night. I could not look at that creep the rest of my time there. He was behind the bar all the time, looking up at me. He had a wonderful family that would come in early in the evening and have dinner. He had a little son, a daughter and a lovely wife. I would have loved to tell her what an asshole she was married to and what he did to me. But I couldn't tell anyone. For one thing, I didn't know who would believe me. I also questioned myself - did I do something wrong? Was there something that was said in a conversation that gave him the wrong impression? He didn't know how old I was. I couldn't tell anybody about it. I was underage, under contract, and had a lot of bookings to get to. It was awful working at that place. I couldn't wait to get out of there.

My arms were so bruised that I had to put that terrible pancake makeup on to hide the bruises. My back was hurt and scratched up from the table. Luckily, no one could see that. I had a bruise on my face also. Thank God for makeup or I would have looked like a prize fighter who lost the fight.

We went to Racine, Wisconsin next and worked the club where Patti Page got her start. After that, we moved on to South

Bend, Indiana. There were lots of good-looking college guys there! Big football players from Notre Dame! While we were in South Bend, we realized that there were some weird laws that we weren't familiar with. One of them was that women were not allowed to sit at the bar and no one could have a drink in their hand unless they were sitting down. If you moved to a different table, the waitress would have to move your drink.

When Lue and I left South Bend, Indiana, we headed to Atlanta, Georgia to perform at the Clairemont Hotel. On our way we decided to drive up to Lookout Mountain in eastern Tennessee. You can see seven states from the top of the mountain. I found an eye-opening surprise when I went to use the restroom. Posted outside the women's restroom were two separate signs. One said "black" and one said "white." That's when I noticed the signs over the drinking fountains that said the same thing. "How awful" I thought. "What is wrong with these people?" I was very upset and very sad. I called my parents and told them that the people in that area were crazy and I wondered how human beings could treat other human beings that way?

We worked at the Claremont Hotel in Atlanta for two weeks and then, another group was booked in once our two-week stay was over. The manager at the hotel bar we were working said he had a friend in Savannah who would like our act. He gave us the name and phone number of his friend who owned a club called the "Sand Bar." We called and he wanted us to drive to

Savannah and meet him. He wanted to know if we would be willing to work cocktail hours, 5pm to 9pm.

On the way to Savannah, we went through Chattanooga, Tennessee. I was shocked by the sight of chain gangs of prisoners along the side of the road! The guards were hitting the men with rifles! It was so frightening! Some of the prisoners would fall down and the guards would kick them in the head! I had nightmares for a long time after seeing that.

We finally arrived in Savannah and worked there for many months. The club was small and intimate, across from a beautiful park. It was an ideal job. We had all day long to go to the beach and most of the evening to do whatever we wanted to do. I loved working cocktail hours. Mr. Gannon, the owner of the club, also provided us with lodging in a beautiful penthouse overlooking another fantastic park. Better still was the fact that we didn't have to pay a booking agent because we were no longer under contract, since we had found the gig through our friend in Atlanta.

All of the service workers at the Sand Bar were black men with white shirts and black ties. They were very classy gentlemen, always polite and treated us very well. In those days, we carried tons of equipment with us. Big amplifiers, guitars, my 48-pound accordion, the whole works. The waiters would always help us to bring our equipment in and help us set it up.

One evening, there was an obnoxious patron in the bar who obviously had too much to drink. I remember he was trying to act like a big shot, buying drinks for his table and being loud. He angrily called the waiter over and started yelling at him, telling him that he messed up one of the drinks. He spit on the waiter's tray and yelled "There is your tip!" It didn't sit right with me, so on break I went and confronted him. I asked him what was wrong with him and told him that he was disgusting for how he acted. Just then, someone tapped me on the arm and told me that Mr. Gannon wanted to see me in his office. I went into his office and he asked me if I knew where I was. I said "Of course I knew where I was" and I didn't understand what he was getting at. He looked at me and said "Do you know you're in Georgia? This is Savannah!" I asked him what it had to do with anything and he replied: "I hired you to play music, I do not want you sticking your nose in my business when it comes to the niggers that work for me." I told him that I was terribly upset that someone would treat an individual the way that customer did. He told me that it was not my business and he would handle it, and if I were to stick my nose in his business again, I would be out of a job. I could not believe his reaction! I didn't like that place very much after that, considering how he had treated me, and how he could let one of his workers be treated so disrespectfully. Especially a waiter who I knew to be a gentleman.

We did meet a lot of nice people during our time in Savannah, though. One night we were performing at the Sand Bar and a group of people came in. During our break, they invited us to sit down with them. They asked us when we would be done working for the night, and we told them that our last set was done around 9 o'clock. They introduced themselves as the Wilburn Brothers, whom I was not familiar with at the time even though they were pretty big country artists. They told us that they were performing a show at the nearby auditorium, and if we wanted to come, they would tell the doorman that they were expecting us. They said we could hang out backstage and meet some of the other performers in the show. We thought it was a great idea! When we got done that night, we went to the auditorium. The show started at 8, so we were a bit late. Just as they had instructed us, we went around to the back and knocked on the door. The doorman greeted us and took us backstage, and we met with the Wilburn Brothers again. Doyle Wilburn introduced me to Ernest Tubb – the headliner of the country show. I was also introduced to Marty Robbins, and I had a couple of pictures taken with some of those guys.

Although I had some good memories that stemmed from our time at the Sand Bar, my feelings about the club were already tainted by Mr. Gannon and how he let the customers treat his employees. We left there after eight months and headed back to the Twin Cities. At this point I was tired of life on the road and very lonesome for my family.

*The Charmettes--Jan North and Lue Brown*

*Jan Sherman*

# Flame Café - (1956-1962)

*Jan North at the Flame Café*

## Ardis Wells & The Rhythm Ranch Girls

After a few weeks at home, I got another call from Mr. Torp. He said he knew a woman in Minneapolis who was looking for a lead player who could also sing. My father and I went to meet her and also see the club where the band played. We told her and the owner that I was not 21 years old. They said it wasn't a problem as long as I didn't drink. I auditioned for them and we reached an agreement. So, there it was: I started rehearsing with Ardis Wells and the Rhythm Ranch Girls. I told them that I just got off the road with another girl who sang great harmony. They decided to get in touch with Lue and hire her, despite the fact there were already more guitar players than we needed. After a couple of weeks, they gave Lue a two-week notice. She wanted me to quit the all-girl band and go back on the road with her. I wasn't interested in doing that again! I politely declined that offer. Several years later, Irene Brown called me and we went to lunch together. She told me that she and her sister, Lue, weren't speaking to each other. That didn't surprise me at all! She also told me that Lue had caused her many problems over the years. During one of their arguments, Lue admitted to Irene that she was the one who had called the police and tried to get me fired from the Midway Gardens where I was working six nights a week. Guess what, it worked! I had to quit working with Irene and I also couldn't sing with the male quartet. Because I had no other option, I had to go on the road with Lue. She ended up trying this same stunt when Ardis Wells gave her a two-week notice. She didn't succeed this time though! The owners knew how old I was, and always protected me. What a snake she turned out to be!

*Fern Dale, Ardis Wells, Patti Williams, and Jan North*

**The History of the Flame Café**

The Flame Cafe hosted some incredibly big name acts during the 40s and 50s: Ella Fitzgerald, Dizzy Gillespie, and Gene Krupa, just to name a few. The last act to appear at the Flame during those years was the Buddy Rich Quintet in July of 1955. The Flame had a cover charge at that time to help cover the expenses of those big-name artists. Sometimes the cover charge didn't quite bring in enough money to cover the expenses, so the club was operating in the red.

Shortly after that time, the Perkins brothers, Ray and Abe, whose actual name was Percanski, decided to try something different. They hired Johnny Tally, who went by the name of Johnny T. He was a disc jockey at KEVE radio and had a small western band. He stayed at the Flame for a short time, and shortly after they hired Jimmy and Ardis Wells. Then Wells had a western swing band that consisted of six musicians. The band was called "The Dakota Roundup." Jimmy Wells was an accordion player and Ardis Wells played rhythm guitar and bass fiddle, sang, and yodeled. Before settling down to play in the band, Ardis had tried her hand at other careers; one of them was that of a professional wrestler. Another time, she rode the elephants in the circus.

Dubbed "the Hillbilly Band," the Dakota Roundup" proved to be successful. Word got around and the crowds started to come and the dining room started to fill up. The Flame Cafe served very good food. A sixteen-ounce T-bone steak selling for $1.50 was the featured item on the menu. After a few months, the Perkins brothers asked Ardis Wells to get a band together to perform in the front cocktail room of the Flame. Within a couple of weeks, she started rehearsing with a couple of girls. One of them was named Princess JoAnn. Her boyfriend, Curly Waldsmith, was playing in the dining room with the Dakota Roundup. Princess JoAnn was a very pretty girl who was partly of Native American ancestry.

Fern Dale was hired to play banjo. She loved the idea of playing six nights a week instead of one-night stands. Barbara

Lee Mac played bass and she sang very well although drinking seemed to be problematic for her. Ardis also hired a girl named Linda Riley, a beautiful red-headed steel guitar player. Her friend, Jolene, was hired to play accordion. Both Linda and Jolene came from Indianapolis, Indiana to play at the Flame. All the girls wore western clothing. It was quite the novelty to have an all-girl band, and soon enough the cocktail lounge was busy and profitable.

The All-Girl band was unique but had its problems. Some of the girls were very opinionated and it wasn't long before some of them left. Jolene went back to Indianapolis, Barbara Lee decided to leave, and Princess JoAnn also quit. Ardis tried rebuilding the band. She hired Patti Weegman who played rhythm guitar and bass. Ardis even hired a man at one point to play lead guitar. His name was Gordy Porter. He didn't stay long because the big attraction was that the band was totally made up of women.

Not long after that, I started playing with Ardis Wells. We rehearsed and played many, many hours together. Especially with the specialty numbers that Fern Dale played on her banjo. When I was on the road with Lue, we didn't play much country music so all of the country music was very new to me. All of us eventually adopted singing roles and ended up performing many duets together. We even sang some four-part harmonies. When Linda Riley left the band to go back to Indianapolis, Ardis hired

Marcy Hall to play lead guitar. Marcy wasn't fond of singing, but she did a few numbers with us. Marcy and I remained very good friends until she passed away in 2014.

The All-Girl Band made a few trips to Chicago to appear on the Pee Wee King TV show. Pee Wee was an accordion player and a great songwriter. One song he wrote was called the "Tennessee Waltz." Another was called "Slowpoke." Ardis Wells got all the girls train tickets to Springfield, Missouri where we performed on the Ozark Jubilee. Red Foley was the emcee of that national TV show. It was a lot of fun for all of us.

I met LeRoy Van Dyke in Springfield. He had a big hit with the "Auctioneer'" song. He was a regular on the Ozark Jubilee and worked a few times with us at the Flame after our appearance on that show. I had the opportunity many years later to meet with LeRoy Van Dyke when he was performing at the Minnesota State Fair. We had a great time reminiscing about our days at the Flame Cafe.

When I was working at the Flame, Ray Perkins would often request the presence of some of the members of the all-girl band to greet certain customers. He also expected us to sit with these customers during our intermission. One day, he summoned me to the dining room to meet one of his friends. He introduced me to a man named Kidd Cann. I had heard rumors that Kidd had mob ties. Oh no! What's a nice girl like me doing in a place like this? I guess his real name was Bloomfeld, but his moniker was Kidd Cann.

Kid Cann was a nice looking, well-dressed man who stood up when I was introduced to him and pulled the chair out so I could sit with him. He asked me if I would like a drink, so I accepted. The waitress knew what I drank, as did the bartenders. It was catawba juice, not to be confused with catawba wine. Because I was underage and hated the taste of anything with alcohol in it, I would always order catawba. Because it was served in a wine glass, the customers always thought I was drinking wine. I'm sure they were always charged wine prices. I made small talk during my visit with Kidd Cann, and he asked me questions about the roads I had travelled earlier in my career. He was very pleasant and said he would see me again soon. I hoped I didn't show how nervous I was.

When I asked Ray why Kidd Cann had that name. He told me that if someone wanted something done in Minneapolis and they couldn't find anyone to do it, they would call him. The saying was if you couldn't find someone to do it, the "Kidd Cann." I guess you can't tell a book by its cover. During my years at the Flame Cafe, whenever Kidd Cann came in, he would talk to Ray then have me come and sit with him during our intermissions. He was always the ultimate gentleman.

I loved being at The Flame with Ardis Wells and her all-girl band, The Rhythm Ranch Girls. I was much more comfortable staying around the cities with my family than I was travelling on the road. One of the girls in the band, Fern Dale,

*Jan North, Patti Williams, Ardis Wells, Fern Dale, and Marcie Hall*

was a fantastic banjo player who had worked with the Andrews Sisters earlier in her career. Gloris Okary, one of our guitarists, played a great lead guitar. Our steel guitar player was Linda

Riley, who was from Indianapolis. Patti Williams, who would become my partner a few years later, played bass and guitar.

Ten years my senior, Patti was married to Vern Weegman. They had met during a gig in Waterloo, Iowa where Vern worked as a DJ. They married and moved to Minneapolis where he found employment at KEVE, a country radio station where he worked both as a DJ and in sales. Their son, Randy, was born in the early 1960s. Five years later they adopted Ricky who is now a sports writer for a Duluth newspaper.

My friend, Marcy Hall, joined the band a while later, playing lead guitar and harmonica. I played my accordion and sometimes drums. All of us sang. We had some great vocal arrangements with three and four-part harmony.

Our outfits were form fitting and full of rhinestones and fringe. We ordered some of them from Nudie in California who also made outfits for the stars that played on the Grand Ol' Opry.

## Ray Perkins, Spumoni, and a Boat That Needed Fixing

The owner of the Flame Cafe was a short, stocky man named Ray Perkins. I first met him to discuss working with the all-girl band. I remember he ordered us all huge platters of spumoni. It had to be close to half a quart of spumoni on each of our plates! Spumoni is an Italian ice cream that has pistachios in it and it was very good, but not in those quantities! He also brought us all glasses of charged water. Ick, who can drink charged water anyways?! I didn't want to hurt his feelings but I couldn't manage to eat it all! He sure did though.

Ray was very protective of the girls in the band - especially me, knowing I was so young. A couple of times, he invited us all to come on his boat with him. He had a large boat that he kept docked on the St. Croix river. One Sunday afternoon, all the girls managed to make it out there on the boat with him. He brought chicken cacciatore. The Flame had quite a menu and he had them make the food for us. We all ate very well every time we were guests on Ray's boat! The Flame was known as "The Home of the 16-Ounce T-bone."

A different time when we were on Ray's boat, something happened to the motor while we were out on the water. I was the only one small enough to crawl down into the lower belly of that thing. I went all the way down on a plank and pushed some buttons, all while visualizing all the terrifying creepy crawlies that could have been down there! After we messed with it for a while, Ray finally got the motor started again. After that episode, I declined any more invitations on his boat because I wasn't sure if I would get back or have to fix the engine again!

**Texas Bill Strength**

Texas Bill Strength was a big personality during the "Flame" years. He was a disc jockey on KEVE radio and had a TV show on a local station. He also had some recordings on Capitol Records that did very well for him. "Yellow Rose of Texas" and

"Cry, Cry, Cry" were a couple of them. Texas Bill booked the major headliners into the Flame Café every week and was also the emcee in the dining room at the Flame. He was good friends with most of the artists he would book in and would interview them on his radio program as well. Some even appeared on his TV show. That was great advertising for The Flame and drew big crowds at the club.

On one occasion he booked Patsy Cline and advertised that she would be her appearing on his television show. Patsy was staying at the Buckingham Hotel off 16th and Nicollet and needed a ride. Texas Bill asked if I would pick her up and bring her to the show. I agreed and at the appointed hour arrived on Patsy's doorstep. Trouble was Patsy had forgotten all about her impending TV appearance and had just washed her hair and put it up in big rollers to let it dry naturally as hair dryers were not a common commodity in those days. What to do? Without missing a beat, Patsy wrapped an elegant chiffon scarf around her head, rollers and all, knotted it in back and off we went. The show must go on.

Texas Bill owned a record shop on 10th and Marquette in Minneapolis. Our all-girl band appeared many times at his shop and did many remote broadcasts from there. It was always crowded in the record shop when live bands were performing. Crowded and very hot!

Bill bought each one of us girls in the all-girl band white Stetson's, beautiful white cowboy hats, and they each had our names embossed in gold inside of the band. I had mine for many years until I was asked to donate it to the Country Music Hall of Fame in the Stearns County Museum in Saint Cloud.

*Texas Bill Strength*

Despite his talent and popularity, Bill had a knack for attracting trouble. One time, he got shot. He was hanging out with Duke Larson, who was a good friend of ours for many years, and a great performer. Bill and Duke were going to meet some friends at an after-hours party. Apparently, they knocked on the wrong door in the middle of the night. The man who owned the house opened the door holding a sawed-off shotgun and shot Texas Bill Strength as he stood on his doorstep hitting Bill just above the knee in-between his legs.

Bill was brought to the Hennepin County Medical Center where he stayed for a long time. I went to visit him and it looked like he had strips of bacon on the insides of his legs where doctors had grafted skin from somewhere else on his body. A group of us got together and held a big benefit for him in Forest Lake to help pay for the huge medical bills he incurred.

In August of 1973 Texas Bill Strength was involved in an accident with Bob McDonald when they were working a show out in the Dakotas. Bill and Bob had rounded a curve too fast and the car ended up rolling. Bill was hurt quite badly and was airlifted to Regions Hospital in Saint Paul. His jaw was wired shut and he had several broken bones.

Again, we gathered a group of musicians and held a couple of benefits to help pay for his medical bills. One was in Forest Lake and one at the Medina Ballroom. I was at the hospital visiting him after this accident when the owner of KEVE radio came in to visit Bill. He told Bill he would build a ramp into the radio station so Bill could get in with his wheelchair when he was ready. A lot of us were quite emotional about that.

As you've probably heard by now, Texas Bill Strength was in a tragic automobile accident August 4th in North Dakota. As a result he is now a quadraplegic, paralyzed and unable to use his arms or legs. The hospital bills are piling up and Bill and his family are facing an uncertain future of no one knows how many years of costly therapy. He's a gutsy guy and deserves to make it but he needs all our help. We're asking everyone who likes or appreciates Country Music to contribute whatever they can to a fellow who helped make Country Music what it is today in the Upper Midwest. Time, Gifts - a kind word - Any or all will be greatly appreciated. Thank You

*Texas Bill Strength Benefit Letter (Sent to Radio Stations)*

43

Unfortunately, Bill developed pneumonia while he was in the hospital, along with a high fever, putting him into isolation. Bill never recovered from his accident. He passed away at Regions Hospital in Saint Paul in October of 1973. His death was a huge loss for the country music community, not only in Minnesota, but nationwide. Bill had a lot of friends in the industry from all around the globe. He certainly was one of the people who put the Twin Cities on the map through booking and organizing country shows. He was a great man and is missed to this day by many people. He would be so proud of his sons, Dale and Bob. They are both great musicians and wonderful young men.

*Texas Bill Strength Medina Ballroom Benefit Flyer*

**Jerry Reed**

Jerry Reed was one of the artists who came to the Flame. The first time he performed there, he was not yet 21 years old. Of course, there I was, 18 years old. Jerry and I got to be very good friends. We had a mutual admiration going on and a lot in common. Most of the other musicians enjoyed smoking and some of them enjoyed drinking. Jerry and I didn't drink. We were not old enough, and we didn't like the taste of it. Jerry was a great entertainer and a very good guitar player.

Every Saturday we would do a live remote broadcast at some business, usually a business that advertised on the local country radio station, KEVE radio in Golden Valley. One time when Jerry was in town we did the remote broadcast together. He didn't have a vehicle. Since I had to go home and change clothes for work that night, I invited him to come with me. My mother always had more than enough food because one of us kids was always dragging a friend home with us to eat. After dinner, Jerry started playing my old guitar for my family. My brothers got the biggest kick out of it and my parents enjoyed it, too.

My mother made pork chops, corn on the cob, mashed potatoes and gravy that night for dinner.. Jerry thought he had died and gone to heaven. Entertainers get so tired of eating in restaurants all the time that it's nice to have a home cooked meal. Jerry really enjoyed the hospitality and meeting my family. He and I got to be very good friends and corresponded for a long time. I still have a shoebox full of love letters from him.

When I went to Nashville for the DJ convention, I got together with Jerry for lunch; then we met up with Chet Atkins and visited a couple of hospitality rooms. Jerry had a guitar that he had borrowed from someplace. He and Chet sat on the beds in the hotel room playing music and picking together. A few other people came in to listen to them I only wish I had had a recording device. They were great friends and Chet taught Jerry Reed a lot.

Jerry went on to become a movie actor starring in "Smoky and the Bandit" with Bert Reynolds and other movies. In later years I had a chance to visit with Jerry when he performed at the Minnesota State Fair and at Mystic Lake Casino. We were buddies.

**Audrey Williams**

Every week at the Flame Café, a different guest artist would come in and perform in the dining room. The artists loved coming there because they could stay in the same place for six nights. We got to know quite a few of them and became good friends with some as well.

Our friend John Smith (his real name) and his wife were always very kind to all the musicians. They had a beautiful home in Golden Valley. Usually on Saturday nights, John and his wife would invite a lot of people to come over, including some of the artists. Some of the musicians would bring their instruments and have a little jam session. They'd always have food and every drink you could imagine. It was a comfortable surrounding and we all really enjoyed their hospitality. One particular Saturday, Audrey Williams joined us. Audrey, who had been married to Hank Williams (also the mother of Hank Williams Junior) was performing with us that week at the Flame Café. Audrey had to leave early in the morning to catch her plane to get back to Nashville but that evening she had a bright idea for a game. We all had to put our shoes in a big pile and then mix them all up. Then, everyone would scramble around and try to find their own pair of shoes. Whoever found their shoes first would be the winner.

A couple of the guys argued and didn't want to take their shoes, actually their cowboy boots, off. Audrey started chasing one of our friends around the huge house in her bare feet, trying to convince him to take his shoes off. As she was running around, she hit a drain spout cutting a large gouge in her big toe. In fact, she actually broke her big toe. Her foot swelled up about three times its normal size. Even though she was in a lot of pain, she wouldn't allow any of us to take her to the emergency room. She just had to get on that plane in the morning. By the time she was ready to leave, her foot was so swollen and sore that she was crying in pain. But still, she left for the airport in the morning and flew home on schedule.

AUDREY WILLIAMS    COMPLIMENTS OF THE FLAME
                   10th & NICOLLET
                   MINNEAPOLIS, MINN.                MGM Records

*Audrey Williams of MGM Records*

**The Lone Ranger**

One night at the Flame, the owner came and said there was a gentleman in the dining room that he would like us to meet. The members of our all-girl band headed back there and he introduced us to a man named Clayton Moore along with Clayton's brother who was an insurance agent in Minneapolis. I wasn't aware of it at the time, but Clayton Moore was actually the Lone Ranger. We sat down and had a nice chat with him and his brother. Clayton told us that he was doing a big show at the

Minneapolis Auditorium the next day. He invited us to come and watch it.

Our band, the Rhythm Ranch Girls, had a radio remote scheduled that day until 11:00, but Claytons' Lone Ranger show didn't start until 1pm. We told him we would do our best to make it. He told us to come around to the back door and he would let security know to let us in. We showed up and made our way inside. Clayton was dressed for the show, but he didn't have his mask on. He was also smoking a cigarette, something he never let the public see him do when he was in his outfit. He took us to see his beautiful stallion, Silver. Silver had a big package hanging down and Clayton was hitting it with a stick to try and calm him down. He seemed to be embarrassed that the horse was aroused by all the showgirls surrounding him.

The Rhythm Ranch Girls also had the opportunity to meet Mr. Weatherwax, who was Lassie's trainer. He was in the same show. There were actually five dogs that looked like Lassie. Mr Weatherwax said certain dogs were better trained to do certain tricks and doing two shows a day was too much for just one dog. We were surprised at how much the dogs differed in size, but I guess the audience didn't notice because they thought there was only one Lassie. We got to watch the whole show. Tonto wasn't there on this trip, it was just the Lone Ranger and Mr. Weatherwax.

## My Big Birthday Cake

While at the Flame one time, it was my birthday and one of the customers bought a cake for me that was five-feet high! It had seven tiers on it. The cake was in the big dining room. It was on a Sunday, because that room was dark on Sunday nights. All the lights were off in the room and when they lit all the candles on this beautiful five-foot tall cake, it was awesome! The cake was decorated with little instruments all the way around. It was absolutely gorgeous, and such a nice surprise for me! We all had a big party after the club had closed for the night. What a wonderful birthday I had that year!.

## Babysitting for Willie Nelson

Willie Nelson performed at the Flame Cafe multiple times while I was there doing shows with Ardis Wells and the Rhythm Ranch Girls. One time, he had two of his children and his girlfriend with him. There wasn't much for kids to do in downtown Minneapolis and it was clear that they were very bored. My friends owned the amusement park and concessions at Como Park, so we took Willie's kids there a couple of times. They enjoyed the zoo, but they were really keen on the rides even though Willie's daughter got sick to her stomach from riding the Tilt-A-Whirl so many times.

*Willie Nelson*

## Pheasant Hunting with Tex Ritter

One week, Tex Ritter came to town to perform at the Flame. Tex had a huge hit song called "High Noon" and he was also in a movie by the same name. Tex had done several cowboy movies throughout his career and he was a wonderful speaker. He could tell stories that kept you on the edge of your seat like no other person I had ever heard.

He liked to hunt and had been on several hunting expeditions all over the world. Tex Ritter toured with a friend of his, Hank Morton, who was a bass player and comedian. Hank and Tex had a funny routine where Hank would say something rude to Tex between songs, so Tex would turn around and pretend to hit him in the mouth. Hank would have a whole mouthful of corn and he'd spit them out like all of his teeth just got knocked out of his head!

Tex wanted to go pheasant hunting during his time in Minnesota — so Ardis Wells, her husband ,Jimmy, a friend of ours named Dick Van Hale, Tex Ritter, and I packed up all of our hunting gear and drove out to Ortonville, Minnesota for this hunting expedition.

It was a Saturday night after we had gotten off work at the Flame. Hank stayed back at the hotel. He told us we were crazy and he was not interested in going out there and tramping through those corn fields, especially after work and with no sleep!

Tex and Hank were staying at a small Holiday Inn on Highway 100 and Highway 55 at that time. So, off we went. Dick Van Hale knew some people in Ortonville who had some cornfields that we could tramp through for pheasants. To make a long story short, we hiked and hiked. Dick was the only one to bag a bird. The rest of us never fired a shot.

When we got back to Minneapolis, we were all pretty tired from staying up all night while we hiked around trying to find pheasants to shoot. Tex Ritter walked into Hank Morton's room and proudly showed him the pheasant he had shot. Then, we noticed that there was another pheasant laying on Hank's bed! Tex asked him where he got it from. Hank said he had shot it right from his hotel window! Hank ribbed us all about that for a long time after that!

Another time when Tex was in town, John Smith had a party at his house in Golden Valley. Tex Ritter told a story to several of us sitting in the basement by a fireplace in John's recreation room. It was about the time he and Hank were out on an Indian reservation in Nevada. Tex said they had just finished up a big show and the chief of one of the tribes invited them to come and be his guest. The chief was loved and well-respected by everyone. Tex said it would have been be rude to turn the chief down, so they accepted. So Tex and Hank went to an event, which was called "Feast of the Virgin" at which one of the tribe members had to sacrifice his oldest daughter, who was a virgin, to be put on a spit and cooked! It would be an honor for the family that had been chosen to give up their firstborn virgin daughter to be served to the rest of the tribe.

While the first-born virgin was cooking, the Indians passed a peace pipe around that the guests were expected to smoke as part of this ceremony. Tex continued telling us all about this huge ritual. Everybody was glued his story as he talked about the tribe in such detail. He told us how they slept in caves, the crazy things they would eat, and some of the other wild things the chief had told them as they were seated next to each other at the ceremony. When dinner was ready, the Indians started to divide up the meat of the virgin amongst the tribe members. By the time it got to Tex and Hank, the only part of the virgin that was left were a couple of burnt, charred fingers.

As it turns out, Tex had made the whole thing up! After that, nobody believed any of his other wild stories!

## Roger Miller and Grandpa Jones Go Fishing

During our time in Nashville, Patti and I became great friends with Roger Miller. He had many hits such as "King of the Road" and wrote many songs for other artists as well. We told Roger about how Grandpa Jones, who was a regular on the national TV show called "Hee-Haw," would always book into Minnesota when it was fishing season then head up to Northern Minnesota in a little camper to go hunting and fishing after his stint at the Flame Café. During the conversation, Roger Miller told us about his own hunting expertise; about the time he had "gotten so high" he could have gone duck hunting with a rake!

## Charlie Hodge and the Marksmen

The dining room at the Flame Café had a large hydraulic stage that went down into the floor so it could be turned into a dance floor. Between the cocktail lounge and the dining room we had about eighteen to twenty musicians performing. One time, we even had two separate bands alternating in the cocktail lounge.

One week, a male quartet, called the Marksmen, came up from Nashville to perform. A couple of them were better known for being part of a group called the Jordanaires, who did backup vocals for Elvis Presley, as well as many other artists. They did fantastic four-part harmony.

One of the men by the name of Charlie Hodge was a great singer and a marvelous musician, although The Marksmen never played any instruments when they were on stage. They didn't need to. The Flame had a whole band in the back room that would back them up. During rehearsals, however, Charlie would play keyboard or rhythm guitar.

I got to be good friends with Charlie. We went for lunch a few times and would have coffee at the club before we got on with our evening of work.

Charlie later went on to become Elvis Presley's musical director and lived at Graceland for seventeen years. We were close for many years and I remember meeting up with him in Nashville a few times. He loved to tell me some of the escapades that he would get into with Elvis and his boys. According to Charlie, one time he was in Germany with Elvis when "the King" started throwing hundred-dollar bills on the ground and handing them out to strangers. They lived pretty recklessly when they were traveling.

I have a picture that Charlie autographed for me. It says "To my darling, my love, my size."

THE MARKSMEN    PERSONAL MANAGEMENT    harmon-myers

*Charlie Hodge and the Marksmen*

## Dale Street Accident

Although Patti and I lived separate lives, we made it a practice to drive to and from work together, for both companionship and safety. One night, coming home from work in Minneapolis, we had stopped to eat. It was very late as we drove east on Highway 36 where the city was putting in a new bridge over Dale Street. As we came down the hill, I could see lights flashing along the side of the road. We thought, at first, that the police might be checking on the equipment being used to construct the bridge. As we got further down the hill, we saw a car upside-down with two doors open, rocking in the middle of the street and spewing smoke. There were no police. We were the first ones on the scene of a terrible accident!

Patti and I stopped and ran to the car. I could hear a baby crying somewhere in the distance. We tried to figure out how many people were in the car and how badly they were injured. A little boy with a ballcap on and a baseball glove in his hand was in the back of the car crying at the top of his lungs and petrified with fear. We found the boy's father laying in the ditch with scratches all over him. I didn't know if he was alive or dead. Then we heard the baby screaming again. Patti followed the sound of the cry into a nearby field, found the screaming baby and picked it up. I put the boy with the baseball glove in my car and wrapped him in a blanket to try and calm him down. Soon we found a woman wandering around. She was the mother of the two children.

Seeing another vehicle off in the distance, we ran over there. The car was badly mangled. Later, we found out that the four in the car were students at the University of Minnesota. Another car came driving up. I told them to drive to a filling station down on Rice Street and call the police. This was before we all had cell phones. It wasn't long before the police and two ambulances arrived at the scene.

We learned that the four young people in the mangled car had been coming home from Wisconsin where the drinking age was 18, enticing so many young people from Minnesota to cross the state line for a night of drinking. The family, from White Bear, Minnesota had been heading to the lake for the weekend, leaving at night so their children could sleep. Turns out, they had forgotten something, so they were going back home to retrieve it. As the father was making a U-turn on Highway 36, the car with the young people in it was coming over the hill. It hit them broadside. The police pronounced the four University students dead at the scene.

I have often thought that if Patti and I hadn't stopped to eat, we would have crossed Dale Street too early to have been on the scene to help these people.

The aftermath of the accident lasted a long time with the insurance companies calling and questioning us because we had been the first people on the scene that day. We tried our best to give them all the information we knew. It was a terrible accident and I had nightmares about it for years to come.

**The UFO**

Another time I was driving around the beltline, also known as Highway 100, in Minneapolis on my way to pick Patti up. We were doing a radio remote show someplace. As I drove along, I looked up in the sky and saw a bright white light. It was zipping all over the place, faster than I had ever seen anything move across the sky. After a while, it turned from white to bright red. I watched it for miles - going up, around, down, all over.

When I got to Patti's house, her small black cocker spaniel was going crazy. He was yelping and running around the house and no matter what Patti did, she couldn't calm him down. I told Patti that I had seen that light flying around, and we both went outside to look for it. We weren't disappointed. We saw it shooting across the sky, then up, then down! It was amazing!

The next day, I told my mother what I had seen. She was not convinced and told me not to tell anyone about it, I assume because she was afraid people would think I was crazy. The following day there was an article in the paper confirming that other people had seen the same phenomenon and had reported it to the airport in Crystal, Minnesota. They said it was a UFO.

## Ray Price Meets Our Bouncer Glen

Ray Price was another giant in the country music field. One New Year's Eve, he was in Minnesota to perform at the Minneapolis Auditorium. Usually, on New Year's Eve, the Flame would lock the doors and not allow anybody else to come in after 1:00 am. The musicians were expected to continue working for another hour and a half after the doors were locked. We all got paid good money to be there, but New Year's Eves made for very long and tiring nights.

Fast forward to about 1:45am. All of the doors were locked up. Once you left the club, you couldn't come back in. However, there was a man outside yelling and banging on the door to the club. We had a huge bouncer at the time named Glen. If Glen stood in front of the doorway, you couldn't see through it because he was so huge. Glen opened the door and the guy explained that he was a friend of the musicians working at the Flame. Glen told them he couldn't let anyone back into the club once they had left. The guy said he hadn't been in there yet, that he had just got done working at the Minneapolis Auditorium. Glen the big bouncer told him he didn't care if he just got done working at the White House, he wasn't coming in! The man asked him to tell Texas Bill Strength, who was the MC at the time, that Ray Price was here. Glen told him he didn't care what his name was and that he better leave before he called the cops!

We didn't find out about it until we had taken our break. None of us were too happy with Glen because he had turned away one of the biggest artists of the time! Texas Bill Strength was in charge of booking acts for the club, so he reached out to Ray Price and tried to book him in. Ray refused and said he didn't care what they would pay him, he would never, ever play there after that incident.

## The Million-Dollar Smile

It was just another night at the Flame Cafe. We were on the bandstand playing when all of a sudden, I saw a man with a million-dollar smile walk through the front door. I'll never forget that smile.

He said his name was Jack. I talked with him a bit during the evening and we ended up going out for coffee later that night. Jack asked me if I'd like to go bowling with him some night, and I told him I would love to. We decided to make it a double date. I brought Patti along and Jack brought one of his friends. We went to a bowling alley not too far from the Flame.

We became great friends and eventually, fell in love and in 1958 we married. We had three beautiful sons in quick succession: 1959, 1960, and 1962. Jack and I enjoyed hunting, fishing, and spending time with our children together.

Jack was the love of my life although we found ourselves drifting apart and after twelve years our marriage ended. Still, we remained good friends until he passed away, leaving the memory of that beautiful smile that walked in the front door of the Flame Cafe on that fateful night..

**Will the Real Don Helms Please Stand Up?**

Another time Don Helms, who was Hank Williams steel guitar player, was at the Flame Café playing with a group one week. He was one of the sidemen in the band. On that particular evening, my husband, Jack, was there. As Don Helms was walking out of the dressing room area from backstage and Jack was walking up the aisle, they bumped into each other. They took one look and were astonished! They had met their doppelganger. They could have been identical twins.

At that time, a show called "Whose Line Is It?" was popular on television. A person's "line" of work would be described and each of three or four contestants would claim to be that person. The contestants were asked questions and the judges would have to guess which one was the real person whose "line" it was. The object of the game was to get the real person to stand up.

Jack and Don Helms decided to mimic the TV show. Jack was on the stage first at the Flame as the show began. He was instructed to sit at the steel guitar and then they had Don Helms come out. Both of them stood in front of the steel guitar as the emcee started playing the music for that game: As "Will the real Don Helms please stand up?" blared over the loudspeaker, Jack would sit down and Don would stand up; then Don would sit down and Jack would stand up! This went on for several minutes. Both wore white shirts with string ties and dark horn-rimmed glasses. Both even had wavy curly hair and receding hairlines. The audience was absolutely hysterical because they looked so much alike.

The two men ended up becoming great friends. Later, when I would run into Don Helms in Nashville, he'd say, "You should come and hang out with me because everybody will think that I'm your husband."

*Don Helms & Jack Sherman*

Their resemblance to each other was short-lived. In later years I saw Don Helms at a couple of country shows in Nashville. He had gained quite a bit of weight and had grown a gray beard. My husband, Jack, was quite the opposite. He had lost quite a bit of weight and became very thin.

## Juggling Babies and Career

My oldest son, Jeff, was born in April of 1959 while I was working at the Flame. I would always take him with me to rehearsals and luncheons. Good thing he was a good baby! I nursed him for almost a year and that proved a bit challenging, but it all worked out, most of the time. One time, Patty and I had a radio remote and the show went a little bit longer than expected. We stayed on the stage and I could feel the warmth of my milk leaking. The front of my western suit was soaked, so I couldn't put my accordion down or else others would see. I also started to smell like sour milk after a little bit. That was a long day! The good news was that my baby was well-fed and very happy.

My middle son, Jody, was born in September of 1960. He was such a happy, healthy, beautiful baby! Patty had her oldest son, Randy, three days before Jody was born. That worked out quite well. We both continued to work for the next six and a half months during our pregnancies. I hid my belly behind my accordion and Patty hid her belly behind her guitar.

My youngest son, Jonny, was born in September of 1962. Another healthy & happy baby boy. His brothers sure loved him! One day, I heard him crying in his crib where I found him buried under a pile of toy cars and trucks. His brothers had wanted to cheer him up and give him something to play with. They sure were generous little boys.

## Summertime

As our sons got a little older, Patty and I would take off work during the summer months. My family would spend months at Lake Augusta in Annandale, Minnesota where we would swim and fish and enjoy the beauty of the lake. My in-laws often joined us. As our sons got older, my husband and I would take them to the boundary waters, where we would camp on an island for about a week at a time. We had some wonderful vacations together.

## Freddie Hart and Uncle Gary

Freddie Hart was another big-name artist we worked with sometimes at the Flame. He became good friends with me and my husband, Jack. Jack and I were going out to eat one night after work, so we asked Freddie if he would like to come with us. On the way back, Jack wanted to stop by his mother's house and introduce her to Freddie. Jack's brother, Gary, was a young guy who played the guitar. Freddie picked up Gary's guitar and played a few tunes for us. Gary was so thrilled that Freddie Hart had played his guitar that I think it encouraged him to continue playing his guitar, which is probably why he has grown to be a great musician.

**Polka Dot Granny**

One time when I was working at the Flame, I got a call from our  emcee, Texas Bill Strength. He asked if I could give an artist a ride. He needed to be taken to the doctor for something. I told him I could take him. I asked where he was staying and what clinic he had an appointment at. I went over and picked this guy up and took him to the doctor. He was embarrassed and told me he had hooked up with a woman known as Polka Dot Granny, an older woman who always wore polka dots. He told me that he had partied with her the night before, and now he was having some "penis problems."

I took him to the clinic under an assumed name, but I don't think it worked too well because he was a recognizable singer who also happened to be a movie actor. I guess after a shot and maybe a follow-up he got better, but he made me promise not to tell anyone and I've kept my promise (for the most part)!

**One of the Hazards of being a Showgirl**

Working at the Flame, we became familiar with a lot of different customers. One set of regulars were a pair of twin brothers. The Flame Café had an area in the back hallway that we used specifically for signing autographs. It used to be a coat check. Each musician had their own professional pictures to autograph and hand out to customers. Many times, customers would ask us to autograph a picture for their children or a relative.

One day at home I found a subpoena waiting for me in the mail instructing me to appear in court. I was confused about what it could even be about. My oldest son, Jeff, was a baby at the time. I didn't have anyone to watch him, so I brought him with me to the courtroom. As soon as I walked in, I recognized the twin brothers from the Flame. It turns out that one of the brothers had come into a large inheritance and had blown through it all.

The judge asked me how much money this guy had spent on me. I was confused and told the judge that I wasn't sure what he was talking about. Apparently, the twin in question had told his brother that he was going to marry an entertainer. He had an autographed picture of me that I must have signed one day at the club just like we did every day. The autograph said, "To Bill, with love." He mistook that autograph as a sign that I was interested in him, and apparently, he had told his brother he was going to marry me. OMG, I was flabbergasted!

I told them I was married, and that my son was even with me in the courtroom. The judge asked me if I had ever received any gifts from this man. I told him I had never accepted a solitary thing from him. although it's possible that he may have bought a round of drinks for all of us one night at the Flame, but that's about it. Our bosses always told us if somebody's going to buy you a drink, you don't need to drink it but you better accept and not take the shingles off the roof.

Overall, it was a sad situation. The brother told me later that his twin had ended up in a mental institution. I told him I felt bad and I'm sorry that I had become a part of what has happened to his family. He said his brother's room had pictures of me plastered on every single wall. He told me that his brother had been obsessed with me. I was really frightened! What a sad situation.

## How I Became an Arson Suspect

Many times, while we were on intermission from our shows in the front cocktail lounge at the Flame, we would head to the back room and do an opening act for whoever the guest artist was for that week. There were wings on the stage where we could check our makeup or freshen up a little bit in the dressing room.

All the girls had purses with them, including myself. On one occasion one of the girls suggested we all put our purses inside my accordion case for safekeeping, which we did before going on stage for our set. When we came off the stage fifteen minutes later, I opened my accordion case to put my accordion away and get our purses out. To my horror I discovered that every single one of our purses were gone! I was sick to my stomach. None of us could believe it. How could this have happened? No one was allowed backstage!

We filed a police report. There were some suspicions about who had stolen our purses, but it was very hard to accuse somebody when you didn't know for sure what had happened.

About four years later, I got a subpoena to appear in Minneapolis court. I went to the detective's office and sat down across the desk from him. That's when I saw it –my brown leather purse that had been stolen out of my accordion case four years prior! The detective asked me where I was on September 18th, four years ago. I told him I didn't even know where I was two weeks ago! He told me that the Shaw Lumber company had been victim to an arsonist and that detectives investigating the fire had found my purse stuffed in-between the pallets of two by fours. My identification was still in my purse when they found it, but everything else was either taken or had fallen out.

I told the detective to look back in the records and he would find that my purse had been stolen from the Flame Café, along with six others. It was interesting to me that they found my purse at the site of an arson and were questioning me about it. I didn't live anywhere near Shaw Lumber Company, nor did I ever know that it even existed.

None of the other girl's purses were ever recovered; mine was the only one and at the scene of an arson fire at that!

## Musicians' Language

One thing that I learned during these years was that musicians have their own language. When we played together we would need to know what key another song was played in or what key someone sang a particular song in. But the difficulty about a lot of the different notes is that they all sound the same when you say them. For example, if I was trying to communicate that we were playing in the key of C, half the time the other musicians would think I said D, E or G. They all sound alike. To solve this problem, we started naming the keys. Instead of the key of G, we would say in the key of George. We had elephant for E, dog for D, and Charlie for C. But sometimes it was intuitive. During the forty years Patti and I worked together we could communicate very well with each other on the stand, many times with just a glance.

# Patti and I Become

# The North Sisters

# (1958-1998)

MARVIN RAINWATER

JULY 2ND IS THE BIRTHDAY OF ONE OF THE GRANDEST GUYS
EVER KNOWN TO COUNTRY MUSIC BUSINESS AND WHO I WANT TO
THANK PERSONALLY FOR GIVING JAN AND PATTI THE GREATEST
BREAK IN THEIR MUSICAL CAREER.
    MARVIN WAS BORN IN WICHITA, KANSAS AND NAMED MARVIN
KARLTON RAINWATER. HE HAS ONE SISTER, PATTY, WHO SINGS
WITH HIM ON TWO OF HIS SONGS AND THREE BROTHERS LIVING.

EVEN AS A YOUNG CHILD
HE LOVED MUSIC AND HIS
MOTHER HELPED HIM SO
MUCH IN HIS LOVE FOR
MUSIC. HE WENT TO
SCHOOL IN WICHITA AND
TO HIGH SCHOOL AND
COLLEGE IN WALLA WALLA,
WASHINGTON. HIS OTHER
PET PAST TIME WAS HORSES
AND HE WAS ALWAYS HAPPY
IF HE COULD HAVE HIS
FOUR LEGGED FRIENDS
AROUND HIM.
    HIS MUSICAL CAREER WAS
CUT SHORT FOR WHILE WHEN
HE WAS IN THE SERVICE OF
OF HIS COUNTRY WHICH HE ENTERED IN 1944. HE LATER MARRIED
HIS CHILDHOOD SWEETHEART, CHARLENE, WHOM HE MET WHEN HE WAS
A LUMBERJACK AND TREE SURGEON IN OREGON. WHERE HE HAD A
THUMB INJURY WHICH ALMOST ENDED HIS MUSIC CAREER.
    BROTHER RAY BECAME MARVIN'S MANAGER AND ON MAY 9, 1955
MARVIN'S BIG BREAK CAME AS HE RECALLS IT — THE ARTHUR
GODFREY SHOW WHERE RAY GOT INTO SUCH A GRAND GABFEST WITH
MR. G. THAT MANY MANY PEOPLE HAVE WONDERED WHY RAY ISN'T
ON TV. INCIDENTLY, IT MIGHT BE SAID THAT IF NOT FOR RAY'S
DEVOTION AND FAITH MARVIN WOULD NOT BE IN THE ENTERTAIN-
MENT BUSINESS TODAY. WELL AS IT CAME OUT MARVIN DID "I
GOTTA GO GET MY BA-BY" AND HE WON WITH HONORS. HE HAD
ALREADY DONE A GUEST APPEARANCE ON OZARK JUBILEE AND THEY
SIGNED HIM AS A REGULAR AND ALSO GOT A MGM RECORDING CONTRACT.
    "GONNA FIND ME A BLUEBIRD" REALLY HELPED HIS BOX OFFICE
THE MOST OF ALL HIS RECORDS.

*Marvin Rainwater in our Fan Club Brochure*

*Jan Sherman*

**Marvin Rainwater and Our First Record Deal**

During my time at the Flame Café with the all-girl band, a singer named Marvin Rainwater was booked in to perform. Billed as "The Singing Indian," he wore a buckskin shirt and a beaded headband. Marvin had a huge hit called "Gonna Find Me a Bluebird" that sold over one million records on MGM Records. Marvin was a big star in England as well.

When Marvin Rainwater came to the Flame, people were lined up around the whole square city block to get in to see him. I remember them starting to line up at noon for the evening show. There was never a cover charge at the club.

A lot of big acts performed at the Flame Café – artists from the Grand Ol' Opry, The Townhall Party in California, and the Ozark Jubilee just to name a few. But, during the years I worked there, I never saw any artist bring in more people than Marvin Rainwater.

Patti and I ended up becoming very good friends with him. At times, he would come and perform in the cocktail lounge with the all-girl band and Patti and I would sing harmony for him. He became familiar with our work and really liked some of our duets.

Marvin took some of our recordings to MGM Records, and the artists and repertoire department invited us to come

75

down to Nashville and meet with them. They offered us our first record deal.

**MGM RECORDS** A DIVISION OF LOEW'S INCORPORATED

1540 BROADWAY
NEW YORK 36, N.Y.
JUDSON 2-2000

April 17th, 1958

Patti Weegman & Jo Ann Northrop
P/K/A Jan and Patti North
2930 North Rice Street,
St. Paul, Minn.

Dear Jan and Patti:

        Enclosed for your files is your fully executed MGM recording contract.

        Best of Luck and let me hear from you.

        Sincerely,

        *Jim Vienneau*
        Jim Vienneau

A few months later, Patti and I flew to Nashville. Marvin was there to meet us, and he rehearsed with us in the hotel room for several hours. I remember him helping us with the harmony and suggesting tips on the recording.

In his travels to England, Marvin sent us gifts, specifically chocolate-covered ants and grasshoppers. They actually tasted like chocolate covered nuts, I rather enjoyed them and I'm sure they were nutritious as well.

In Nashville, we recorded at the Owen-Bradley Studios. Floyd Kramer played the piano with us there. He had a huge instrumental song called "The Last Date." Hank Garland was the lead guitar player on our session. He had a big hit with the instrumental, "The Shotgun Boogie". We also had a steel guitar player with us named Jimmy Day. He was Ray Price's steel guitar man. He recorded on all his records and traveled on the road doing shows with him. We also had a studio drummer and a studio bass man.

Patti and I recorded everything at one sitting. We each had our own microphone and big soundboards between us and the other musicians. There was no stereo. Everything was recorded monaurally at the time. While we were listening to our playback, Johnny Cash and some of his musicians were shooting craps in the back waiting for their turn to record. They had the next rental slot at the studio.

Our first record was called "Lonely Moonlight", and we had three takes in the studio to get it recorded. For the "B" side of the record, we only had two takes. That song was called "Sitting and Thinking." The A&R man asked us if we sang any old standards. We sang several for him, and he really liked one we did called "My Happiness." We recorded that on the session, and it ended up being a great cut. They told us they were going to put it "In the Can", so it would be ready for our next release. Our record, "Lonely Moonlight," did well – it broke the top 40 in Billboard Magazine and we were voted the "Most Likely Duo to Succeed" in that issue.

Several months later, as I was listening to the radio, I heard the D.J. announce "My Happiness." But it wasn't our voices I heard. They had been replaced with the voice of Connie Francis. I couldn't believe it! She had recorded the song using our arrangement, overlaying her voice and singing harmony as well..

We had a big fallout with MGM Records over that, but we were bound by their four-year recording contract. MGM Records made it clear that if we recorded anything, we would be sued for breach of contract. So, we waited it out. Our hands were tied.

After the four-year contract ran out, we got a call from our friend Roy Drusky, who was well established as a songwriter and producer in Nashville. He helped us sign another record contract, this time with Briar International. We did release some records that got pretty good airplay in the five-state area. That being said, Briar International did not have the same worldwide reach and brand recognition as MGM. In fact, our MGM recording of "Lonely Moonlight" had done exceptionally well in Germany after it was released, probably due to all the American servicemen that were over there.

Roy Drusky and his wife Bobbie were very good friends of ours. Roy helped Patti and me rewrite some of the lyrics to songs we recorded for Briar International, recording them at Owen-Bradley Studios again. We recorded and cut a lot of tunes in Nashville with some marvelous musicians.

One time during our MGM days, Patty and I flew to Nashville to go to a big broadcast dinner. It was quite expensive. MGM had purchased our tickets. When we arrived in Nashville, I found out that the airline had lost my luggage. What to do? I didn't have anything to wear! The big dinner and ceremony was that night.

We went to Roy and Bobbie's house, and I told her what had happened with the airlines losing my luggage. Bobbie said I could wear her wedding dress, a gorgeous pink lace dress. She was about the same size as me, but a little bit taller. Luckily, Roy and Bobbie had a maid who was willing to alter the dress. Bobbie had me try it on and told me she would be able to hem it up for me. She was very talented and shortened the dress without a problem. I ended up making it to the ceremony in style in that special dress. On top of that Eddie Arnold sat at our table and complimented me on how nice I looked. If he only knew!

*The North Sisters--Patti Weegman and Jan North*

*Jan Sherman*

# RICE STREET GIRL MAKES TOPS IN FIELD OF RECORDED MUSIC

Jan (Jo Ann Northrop) shown on the left in the above picture, daughter of Mr. and Mrs. Harley Northrop, 2930 North Rice, has made "bigtime" in records.

Teamed up with a Minneapolis girl and known as the North Sisters, Jan's first big record on MGM label, titled "Lonely Moonlight" on one side and "I'll Never be Sorry" on the other is selling like hot cakes at record stores.

Jo Ann Northrop, attended Little Canada School, and participated in many musicals under the direction of Mrs. Diane Williams. She attended Alexander Ramsey High School, and is a member of Lakeview Lutheran Church.

playing it quite often, as these are local girls we're hoping that every one buys a record and joins the fan club. The girls made a TV appearance on Tuesday, April 29th at 4:39 on Mary Jo Tierney's program, on Channel 9.

Anyone interested in joining The North Sister Fan Club, may send $1.00 to Ann Kachn, President, 2517 23rd Ave. So., Minneapolis 4, Minn. You will receive a membership card, picture, 5 newsletters and a years end journal.

# SWEET ADELINES WILL BE HEARD MAY 10th

The St. Paul Chapter of Sweet Adelines, Inc. under the direction of Hollis Johnson is making plans for their first annual show entitled "100 Years in Melody" to be presented in the Central high school auditorium on Saturday evening, May 10th at 8:00 p. m.

This is to be a benefit show with all proceeds going to the "Minnesota Society for Crippled Children and Adults" to help buy wheelchairs for crippled persons.

Special guest appearance will be the "Chord Queens" from De Moines, Iowa who are Sweet Adeline International Medalists of 1957.

Rehearsals are held the 2nd and 4th Tuesdays of every month at 8:00 p. m. at the Riverview Commercial Club, 72 Concord.

## RUMMAGE SALE

The Willing Workers Society, of Trinity Lutheran Church, Rice and Aurora, will hold a Rummage Sale at Dietsch's Hall, Thomas and Western Avenues, on May 14th. Doors will open at 10:00 a. m.

Be still prepared for death; and death or life shall thereby be the sweeter.—Shakespeare.

# NEW CAR LOANS

$4.00 Per Hundred Per Year

CAPITAL CITY STATE BANK

*Hometown Newspaper*

**Our Fan Club**

When "Lonely Moonlight" was released on MGM records, our fan club president, Ann Kaehn, contacted all the country radio stations to request they play our recording. She was very familiar with what stations to contact because her husband, Dick, was the head of Jeannie Shepard's fan club and they both had lots of experience.

We sure beat the pavement in those days. Patti and I drove to many, many, small towns and visited many small radio stations. Sometimes they would interview us and play our recordings. Others would take a copy of the recording and play it at a later date. We got to be friends with many of the disc jockeys and radio managers.

Ann became a friend in another special and very supportive way. By 1962 I had given birth to three lively little boys. I could care for them during the day between naps, but when my husband, or mother weren't available evenings to take care of the boys when I worked the clubs, Ann graciously volunteered to babysit. She was a godsend.

In time Ann Kaehn became ill and couldn't continue the workload of our fan club. Patti and I met a young woman who was a good customer and liked our music. We approached her about heading up our fan club. Jan Cierzan was a great help and we became great friends.

*Cover of Fan Club Brochure by Jan Cierzan*

## Down Hookem-cow Way

Patti and I became a duet after we left the all-girl band at the Flame. Our first job as a duo was at a club called the "Hook 'em Cow" in South Saint Paul, Minnesota. The club had tried entertainment for a while and it never worked out. But Patti and I decided we were going to give it a try as a duet. We made a lot of music; we played instruments and we both sang and did harmony numbers. We also gave ourselves a raise. We had worked for scale for a very long time; now we doubled that.

It was a fun place to work. Swift and Company and all of the stockyards were going strong and making big money. When the workers from the meatpacking plants and the truck drivers from all over the US heard there was country music in the Hook'em, we started to really have some great crowds. We packed the place! They built us a new stage and even put in a small dance floor! When we started, we were working two nights a week. It was going so well that the owner asked us if we could switch to performing four nights a week, which we did for four years running.

## Murder at the Stockman Cafe

When Patti and I worked at the Hook-Em-Cow in South Saint Paul, we met a lot of really nice people. The stockyards were busy, and a lot of people who worked there would come in for a good time. Among them was a group of lovely women who came in after bowling each week. One night, our group went to the

Stockman Cafe together. One of the men who had been dancing with the ladies decided to take one of them out to his car for a while. It was a beautiful red mustang. I always envied him for having that car because I really, really liked it. When we had finished eating, the man came back into the restaurant and told us that the woman was not feeling well and was sleeping in the back seat of his red mustang. He had a bite to eat and chatted with us for a while. I remember he had an unusual appearance. The tops of his ears were missing. The story was that a husband had found him in bed with his wife and cut his ears off for revenge.

When the ladies of the bowling team were ready to leave for the night, they went to get their friend from the mustang, but they couldn't wake her up. They called the police who came and pronounced her dead. Apparently, she had gotten sick and thrown up. To this day, I believe the cut-ear man sexually assaulted and murdered the woman. I was good friends with the officer on the case. He had told me that they found semen in her vomit when they tested it. She was the mother of four children and her husband was a well-known politician in Saint Paul. Her death was a terrible tragedy. The man with the red mustang and the lopped-off ears was never charged for her murder. The police kept the story under wraps, likely to protect the reputation of her husband and family. How sad!

## Elvis Presley's Manager

Once when Patti and I were in Nashville for a recording session, we stayed at the Andrew Jackson hotel. That morning, we went downstairs to the coffee shop. Colonel Tom Parker, who was Elvis Presley's manager, came over and sat down with us to chat and drink his coffee, spilling the first cup all over the front of his white shirt. Just then Marty Robbins, another big country name, walked in. Marty climbed up onto a small pedestal where there was a baby grand piano and played a few songs. I didn't know he could play piano; all I ever saw him play was guitar. He played very well and entertained us for a half hour.

## The Grand Ol' Opry

Patti and I loved visiting the Opry when we were in Nashville recording our songs for MGM or Briar International. We had a lot of friends who performed on the Opry. Most of them had visited the Flame Cafe so we had already spent time working alongside them. Sometimes, we would go and hang out backstage. Every Saturday night different artists would perform. One of the nights when we were backstage, someone approached us and asked if we wanted to go onstage and do a few numbers. What a fantastic opportunity! There we were, singing on stage at the Ryman Auditorium! The sound and acoustics were wonderful. We didn't have our instruments with us, so we grabbed a couple guitars and went out and sang our MGM hit, "Lonely Moonlight." We were offered an opportunity to perform and travel with members of the Opry, but it meant committing to many weeks on the road. We were not interested in that schedule. We couldn't relocate because we both had families back home. Perhaps we missed a big chance, but I wouldn't have changed it for anything.

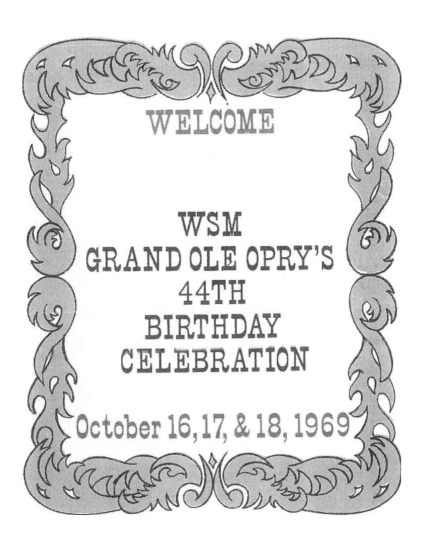

## Hometown Friends Make it Big in Nashville

Jimmy Colvard was a studio musician and one of the finest lead guitar players in Nashville. He grew up in Little Canada and attended the same school as me, but he was a few years younger. He was a good friend to my younger brothers. Jimmy traveled with Rex Allen when he was a young guy and he made quite a name for himself. We always enjoyed seeing him when we got to Nashville and he always liked to talk and reminisce about home and all the friends that we both knew. Jimmy was there to pick Patti and me up at the airport every time we flew to Nashville. What a guy! Sadly, Jimmy committed suicide later in his life.

Another good friend and musician from Little Canada was a guy named Benny Heilman. Benny was a fantastic steel guitar player. He worked with Dave Dudley and then he was part of the Dakota Roundup in the main dining room at the Flame Café. Benny really made a name for himself in Nashville with an amplifier that he designed and built. They were called Heilman amps. Many of the studio musicians had one and they loved those amplifiers! Benny and his wife had many kids. My sister Pat used to babysit for them.

Hal Rugg was another steel guitar player who worked the Flame after Benny Heilman left. He also moved to Nashville and became a studio musician.

**Local Shows after our MGM Debut**

When our "Lonely Moonlight" record was on the Billboard charts breaking the top 40, Patti and I were offered opportunities to perform on a lot of local shows. One of these shows took place at the old Met Center, which used to sit where the Mall of America sits today. We had a big country show out there with Jim Reeves. "Gentleman Jim" Reeves was his nickname. He had a soft voice and sang wonderful country songs. Jim had a major hit called, "He'll Have To Go." Faron Young was also on the show. He was a great entertainer with many hits on the country charts.

We were booked as a backup at this Jim Reeves Met Center event in case one of the acts could not go on. The Musician's Union paid us to be on standby, whether we ended up being in the show or not. Patti and I shared a dressing room with Skeeter Davis. She had a popular song at that time called, "The End of the World."

Since the Met Center was also used for sports, our stage was set up where the pitcher's mound was located on game days. Each act used a house band from the Twin Cities to back them.

When the Jim Reeves show started, a bunch of spotlights were shining on the stage, drawing tons of mosquitoes. When Skeeter Davis went on stage, she inhaled a mosquito, and she couldn't sing! The bug was stuck in her throat and there she was, gagging on stage! A very embarrassed Skeeter came running back into the dressing room, telling us she had a mosquito in her throat and didn't know what to do. I told her she would either need to drink something and swallow the mosquito or try to cough it out. When I suggested that, she started gagging because it nauseated her to think that a mosquito was going to go down into her stomach. Eventually, she managed to get the mosquito up out of her throat and went on to perform a really good show, although she was a mess from coughing and gagging so hard.

After that, Jim Reeves told a joke that was a little bit too racy for the family audiences there. It was noted. The next day, the Minneapolis paper said that he was no "Gentleman Jim" as his nickname implied.

**Dust Storm in Saint Peter**

One unforgettable road show took place in a big theater in Saint Peter, Minnesota. Patti and I were booked for a five-show series with Texas Bill Strength, our old buddy from back in our Flame Room days, and George Jones. The theater was very conventional, with huge curtains that opened at the beginning of a set; then closed at the end.

While Patti and I were setting up our equipment for the show that night, George and Bill decided to go out for drinks. We were still setting up when they returned. All of a sudden, they got into a wrestling match and started roughhousing around backstage. Ignoring them, we continued setting up our equipment. Then they got tangled up in the big heavy purple velvet curtains covering the stage and managed to pull down the entire curtain, along with the rod on top of them! The curtains were so dirty and full of dust that it looked like there was smoke coming up from the stage. The audience started to run from the theater thinking that the whole place was on fire!

Patti and I tried our best to get the wrestling team off the stage and get our equipment set up so we could do the show. The owner of the theater was not happy at all, but somehow, we still managed to get paid for the night although we never got called back to play a show in Saint Peter again!

**Panther Piss**

Another great venue that we worked frequently after our MGM debut was the Lake Marion Ballroom in Hutchinson, Minnesota which offered a great family setting where you could come and listen to live musical performances. During one show, Patti and I were performing with our old friend from the Flame, Texas Bill Strength, who was the emcee for many of the shows we did there. Texas Bill was a huge personality in the industry, gaining most of his popularity from his hit, "The Yellow Rose of Texas."

During one particular show when people were gathered around the stage, Bill grabbed a drink out of a nearby woman's hands and proceeded to take a swig of it. He quickly spit it out and yelled into the mic that it tasted like panther piss! I was so embarrassed that I could have died! That was so inappropriate.

There were children in the audience and Bill had had too much to drink that night.

After that set was over, Bill walked outside. I went flying out the door after him and gave him a shove. He landed in the snowbank. I screamed at him, telling him how embarrassing it was for the entire group to be associated with him after that comment. I told him I would never book another show with him. We finished out the show that night with a lot of tension. Bill tried to be professional about it, but it was too little too late as far as I was concerned.

Lake Marion Ballroom had a reputation for being haunted! There were reports of people seeing ghosts dancing in the Ballroom during the early morning. This wasn't just a one-time thing. Many reputable residents of that area stated that they had seen eerie figures and ghosts many times in there. I'm glad I never saw one.

Dancers always said that the floor at Lake Marian ballroom was the best they'd ever danced on. We worked many shows there with a man named George Hamilton IV. He was a sweet man who was always very gracious. His biggest hit was a song called, "A Rose and a Baby Ruth." That recording was a crossover, ranking in the pop charts as well as the country charts.

Unfortunately, a fire destroyed the Lake Marion Ballroom. A new one was built but it never had the same sound or feel as the original one. I wonder if the ghosts are still around.

*Jan Sherman*

**The Mysterious Click**

Musicians aren't always on stage, entertaining in the limelight. We are often called on to do studio work to back up other musicians who are recording. I was hired to do back-up as a studio musician on several occasions at Sound 80 and Kay Banks Studio in Minneapolis. One of those recording sessions was with Bob Larson, a singer who also yodeled and was a world champion whistler. Bob played the autoharp and performed for children's hospitals and senior residents.

One of Bob's big hits was a song he had written about a centipede with a cast on its broken leg. It was called, "99 Legs and a Thump." I was part of a group of musicians in the studio, playing keyboard for the recording, but all was not going well. A clicking sound was coming through the audio.

The sound engineer tested each of the musicians' mikes trying to determine who was responsible for that irritating click, with no luck. He couldn't find the culprit, so he went back to his sound cave to ponder the problem. Suddenly, he emerged from his sound room, fingernail clippers in hand and confronted me! He handed me the clippers and said, "Cut your nails!" He had solved the mystery. It was my long fingernails clicking on the keyboard as I played that was causing the problem.

**Working the Weekends**

Many of the gigs we worked were on Friday and Saturday evenings; others were six nights a week. We almost always booked a two-week contract with an option where, if the club wanted us longer, we could stay, but also we had the option to leave. We were fortunate to have long engagements at some of the places we performed. One of those venues was The Paddock in Crystal, Minnesota where we played for six years.

*Jan and Patti*

**The Sofitel Hotel Card Game**

Another interesting venue Patti and I worked at in the Twin Cities was a hotel called the Sofitel. Located off 494 in the south metro, it was a large hotel, big enough to host huge conventions. We were hired to play there one night, so we set up shop in one of the convention rooms.

It was all men at this convention with three or four waitresses serving drinks all night long while we played background music. About halfway through the evening, two women walked in. They would approach the men and ask them if they would like to buy a card out of the deck they were holding for $5. Then, the women would tear the card in half, putting half of it in a container and handing the other half back to the man who had bought it. After all the cards had been bought, the women would draw a card at random from the 52 in the container. Whoever had the matching card would redeem it by going into the bathroom with one of the women, I assumed it was to receive some type of sexual favor.

The women repeated this game several times. When Patti and I finally realized what was going on, we told the man who had hired us that either these women had to leave, or we would pack up and go. We were only about halfway through the evening at this point, so he told the two women to leave. When the men's group asked about hiring us for the same event next year, we declined and told them they should find someone else. We never did work that convention again.

### "Mom and Daddy's Polka"

Patti and I cut a few more recordings that had some success here in the five-state region. Patti was a great writer. I could spit out an idea to her and she would turn around and write an entire song about it. When we performed at the local clubs, my parents came down and would watch our shows. They loved to dance the polka together, so Patti wrote a song called "Mom and Daddy's Polka."

One time when we performed the song during a show at Lake Marion Ballroom, we were approached by a man named Ralph Hutmacker. He was the director of a 16-piece band in Minneapolis that played ballrooms around the state. Ralph told us he wanted to record "Mom and Daddy's Polka" with his band. We obliged, and he wrote a score for his band and had them record it. After he had done that, it got some airplay on some of the local radio stations.

Ralph decided he liked the lyrics to it and wanted us to record our vocals along with his band's recording. The only issue was that we didn't sing it in the same key that his band had recorded it in. Ralph transposed the music for each of the instruments in his orchestra and we recorded the song with our vocals on it. "Mom and Daddy's Polka" ended up getting a tremendous amount of play in Minnesota and surrounding areas. It was number one on KNUJ, which was one of the larger radio stations in Minnesota.

Every year, KNUJ hosted a huge celebration called the Polka Day Parade. They hired a lot of the big polka bands to come out and play polka music in New Ulm, Minnesota. The radio station asked Patti and me if we would like to be the grand marshals of the Polka Day Parade. We were extremely honored to be a part of the celebration, let alone grand marshals in the parade! It was wonderful!

We rode in quite a few parades over the years. One of them was at the Rush County Fair in Pine City, Minnesota. The parade was held in August, when the mosquito population was in full bloom. Patti and I were also scheduled to do a twenty-minute show at their grandstand. There were big lights surrounding the whole stage. When it was our turn to go on, you could see swarms of mosquitoes flying around those lights. Hordes of them! Patti and I got up on the stage and started our performance. We wore dresses that had small straps over the shoulders leaving our shoulders and backs pretty much bare, not to mention our arms and legs. The second we got up on stage, the mosquitoes had a heyday! It was absolutely miserable. While we're trying to perform a good set, the mosquitos were all over us! They bit us up on our backs and legs. They flew up our noses and into our mouths while we sang! It was absolutely horrible.

We were asked to come back to the Rush County Fair again, but we respectfully declined the invitation due to the hell-of-a-time we had fighting the mosquitoes there. No thank you!

## The Texas Playgirls

I got a call one day from my friend, Linda Riley, who had played steel guitar in Ardis Wells' band with me at the Flame. She said she had booked her group, The Texas Playgirls, into Harvey's in Lake Tahoe. Apparently, her piano player had walked out on the job. She asked me to fly down there and help her out, since she had promised a four-piece band. She bought me an airplane ticket, and the next day I was on a flight to Lake Tahoe. I took my accordion with me, setting it on the seat next to me on the airplane. I didn't want to check it and have it mishandled by the luggage carriers.

I met Linda and tried on wardrobe. It consisted of tight-fitting pantsuits Luckily, I fit into the costumes worn by the pianist who had walked out. The drummer was a great musician and a wonderful singer, Jerilynn was a young bass player who also played with us. She loved Hank Williams and sang all his songs.

The entertainment at Harvey's started at 5pm in the afternoon and continued until 5am the next morning. There were several groups and we rotated with them every 45 minutes. We needed identification to get downstairs into our dressing rooms, because there had been a bomb threat at Harvey's three months before. With a 15 minute intermission in between the acts, we had seven and a half minutes to get our equipment off the stage and the next act had seven and a half minutes to get their equipment on and set up. Every night, we worked a different schedule and did a rotation with new acts.

There were four major casinos in Lake Tahoe at that time. Liza Minelli was at Harrah's performing across the street. One night, we went to her show and had dinner. Her show was fantastic. Afterwards, we had a chance to go backstage and meet Liza Minelli.

*The Texas Playgirls - Kathy, Linda, Jerelyn, & Jan*

*Left to Right: Jerelyn, Kathy, Jan, Linda*

*Linda, Kathy, Jan, & Jerelyn*

## Royalties and Radio Play

Patty and I received many royalty checks throughout the years. Every time one of our songs was played on the radio, we received a certain percentage of the revenue. Our first recording, "Lonely Moonlight," was number one in Little Rock, Arkansas for about seven weeks. It also sold very well in Germany. Our first record was in the top forty in Billboard Magazine! We were fortunate that KEVE played our recordings and they put out a listing each week of the top records. Some of our records were in their top ten many times. We even recorded some commercials for KEVE radio. A few times, we didn't have a drummer, so we took out our big leather purses and slapped them. The reverb made the purses sound like a drum.

We worked remote broadcasts for KEVE at many locations throughout the Twin City area. Almost every weekend, it seemed like we were doing a live remote show. The remote broadcasts always drew large crowds. It was fun meeting the families that would come to see us. We would autograph pictures and give away treats at some of the locations. I loved seeing the little children, maybe we gave them some encouragement to play an instrument!

## Audited by the IRS

During one of the years I was performing, I made an appointment with my taxman to file my taxes. I told him all the things I had bought for my show (wardrobe, make-up, equipment). During that time, I also made a lot of our costumes because we couldn't always find what we were looking for at local stores.

A few months later after filing my taxes, I got a call from the IRS. They told me that I needed to make an appointment with them as soon as possible to discuss my most recent tax return.

I went down to the office in Saint Paul where an auditor questioned me about my expenses. He told me I couldn't deduct the money I had spent on my wardrobe because the clothes in it could be worn for other purposes as well as for work. Little did he know, you don't wear clothes covered in rhinestones and sequins to church or a PTA meeting! I told him I would go home and get my receipts for the wardrobe and bring in some of the costumes so he could see what I meant.

I made another appointment and headed back with my shoebox full of receipts and some pieces of my performing wardrobe full of fringe, sequins, and rhinestones. I explained that these costumes were used only when I was onstage. The auditor asked where I got my dresses, and I told him that I had made most of them myself. He was impressed. By the end of my audit I had come out quite well with the IRS!

# 1998 - Retirement & Beyond

*Tales of a Country Showgirl*

## Midwest Rock and Country Hall of Fame

The Midwest Rock and Country Hall of Fame event was a very fun time. The year was 2005 and I was surrounded by all of my family and friends. Two very talented men, Doug Spartz and Gene Jurek worked tirelessly to put on the annual Hall of Fame extravaganza at Medina Ballroom in Hamel, Minnesota. There were tons of artists from the five-state area as well as major artists from the Opry. What made it more fun and meaningful for me was that the North Sisters were to be inducted into the Midwest Rock and Country Hall of Fame at the event. Patti and I were to be recognized for our dedication and service to the music recording and entertainment industry as well as our contribution to the history of Minnesota music and being the only artists from Minnesota to have a recording contract on a major label.

Doug's wife, Cindy, did an outstanding job managing the event and keeping everything on track. Getting that done isn't such an easy task when you're dealing with temperamental artists and trying to keep the show moving. Cindy was a superwoman. She kept everything under control and soothed the egos of the fragile.

I was so proud and happy that my family and some of my grandchildren were there for that wonderful evening. Many friends came as well. It was so special.

My other half of the North Sisters, Patti, was in a nursing home and couldn't attend the event. I felt very bad about that. I performed with Sherwin Linton's band and Pam Linton sang harmony with me. She did a great job, but it wasn't quite the same as performing with Patti. My friend Marcy, a great guitar player, came with me as well and played guitar during our performance. It was a huge honor to be a part of the event.

Ironically, the last song that Patti and I ever sang together was "My Happiness." Marci and I went to visit her in the nursing home. We brought a guitar and a small twelve base accordion with us. Patti was on oxygen and was having difficulty breathing, but she managed to sing a few songs with me for old time's sake.

One of the nurses heard us when she walked by and asked if Patti and I could sing in the dining room while they served lunch. We told her we would love to, and they set up an area and microphone for us. We did several sing-a-long songs that the residents knew. They really seemed to enjoy it. Patti and I sang our last song together that day, "My Happiness." Patti couldn't help but cry most of the way through it. I was so happy to be able to spend that time with her because she passed away a few months later.

We had shared so many memories over the years. We laughed, we cried, we watched our babies grow. Patti's husband, Vern, had been a disc jockey at KEVE radio for many years. They had two wonderful sons, Randy and Ricky. I saw Randy frequently after Patti passed away. Sadly, Randy passed away of cancer. Her son, Ricky, lives in Duluth and is a writer for the local paper there.

We recorded this hymn, but it was never released. Patti's sons had it played at her funeral. It is one of many hymns she wrote. These are the lyrics to the bridge of "Never Alone":

*Never alone if you take time to pray*
*Never alone, He'll show you the way*
*When burdens grow heavy and you can't go on*
*Just say a prayer and you're never alone*

**Minnesota Music History Channel**

It was an honor to be recognized by the Minnesota Music History Channel in an article featuring 20 pioneering women in Minnesota music. The Andrews sisters were also featured as was Judy Garland and my dear friend, Jeannie Arlen Peterson. There were a lot of great jazz singers and musicians who were recognized, too. The all-girl band with Ardis Wells was part of it and Patti and I were also listed as one of the 20 pioneers. My grandkids joked that I was good enough to make the list twice.

**Women's Auxiliary of the Metropolitan Musicians' Association**

Being a member and past president of WAMMA was an extremely rewarding experience. WAMMA stood for Women's Auxiliary of the Metropolitan Musician's Association. Our purpose was to promote education to further the musical careers of young musicians. These talented young musicians would compete in our annual scholarship competition at the McPhail

School of Music in downtown Minneapolis. We hired judges who were musicians with the Minneapolis Symphony Orchestra.

The competitors were judged on their appearance, stage presence, and their interpretation and performance of the composition they were playing. They had to memorize their selection and couldn't use any sheet music. Several categories of instruments were present such as brass, percussion, strings, and keyboard.

It was amazing to listen to the performances of these young musicians. No one except the judges, the competitor, and a few WAMMA members were allowed in the room during their performances. Many of the winners went on to further their music education at the Juilliard School of Music in New York City.

WAMMA was not a huge organization, and many of our members were retired musicians. We were operating on a shoestring budget in those years. We held annual style shows to raise funds for scholarships to be awarded to high school seniors. We all put in many hours to plan the style shows. We had to secure a place to have it, plan for models, ticket sales, seating, advertisement, and entertainment for the event. Also, we had to figure out what we had to serve that day. A few members, as well as a couple of my granddaughters and nieces served as beautiful models for the event.

One year, we didn't have enough money in the budget for scholarships. Each of the WAMMA members took thirty dollars out of her pocket so we would have enough cash to pay the third-place winner.

WAMMA received a letter from an attorney. He wanted us to have a meeting in his office. A few of us were afraid that we might be sued for discrimination as we had a very large, diversified group of kids competing for the scholarship funds. Instead, the attorney informed us that a former member of WAMMA had passed away and had left us half of her estate in the amount of $210,000. We were ecstatic. That meant we wouldn't have to dig in our pockets anymore to pay the winners.

A few years after that windfall, our membership was dwindling so we met with the Musician's Union. They agreed to continue the music competition and award scholarship funds. We gave our remaining funds to the union for that purpose.

I still stay in contact with a few members of WAMMA. One of those individuals is my dear friend, Sue Nelson, who plays the organ for the Minnesota Twins at Target Field. I sometimes see her at baseball games, and we reminisce about our days at WAMMA. Jeannie Arlen Peterson and her daughter Patty were longtime members also. They performed many times at our monthly meetings. Jeannie played at my mother's funeral as well. Unfortunately, she has now passed away.

*Jan Sherman*

## Judy and Other Lifelong Friends

My friend, Judy, was a waitress at the Horseshoe Bar where she met her husband Russ, who was known as the pool shark around those parts. Patti and I were booked there when I met my forever-friend Mickey the bartender. Somehow, our paths have all crossed and we have been able to enjoy each other's friendships for a very long time.

After we stopped working together, golfing became a common bond for us. Over the years, we have enjoyed many vacations together as well. We all decided we couldn't take the cold Minnesota winters anymore, so we now travel to beautiful Arizona during the cold months.

Sadly, Russ suffered a bad fall on a job and died as a result of his injuries, so he is no longer with us. Since his passing Judy and I often refer to ourselves as Thelma and Louise since we've shared so many trips together: Alaska, Europe, Mexico, California, and just about everywhere in-between. We have had some crazy times during our travels together.

One time, Judy and I were golfing in a state tournament in northern Minnesota when we encountered a horse trotting down the middle of the highway. Nobody was riding it. We decided to stop at a nearby farm to let somebody know so they could get the horse off the roadway. We pulled into the driveway,

113

but nobody was home. We went to the farm next door, but still no luck finding anyone. Then, as we were pulling out of the driveway, the horse came over and stood in the grass near us. We figured he lived there. Then, he started pawing at the ground with his head down. Then, he started chasing our car! That crazy horse chased us all over town! Taking evasive action, we turned on a dirt road, the dust kicked up by our car must have been too much for him and he wandered off into the brush and left us alone. Close call! Crazy damn horse!

## Jamming with Dave Grohl and The Foo Fighters

During a trip back from Alexandria, Minnesota where my longtime friend and guitarist Marcy and I had been visiting Ardis Wells, we stopped at the Pine Tree Apple Orchard. Marcy wanted to buy a frozen apple pie and I can't pass up caramel apples.

We heard some guitars being tuned up behind a blockade, so we decided to jump the ropes and see what was going on. Sure enough, in one of the outbuildings, we came across some guys who were setting up their equipment. When we went in to talk with them two women came over to tell us we couldn't be in there. One of the guys said, "No it's okay, they're with us,"

They had a couple of nice Fender guitars and a piggyback amp like we had. We told them we have guitars just like that in our car and that we just got back from playing at a nursing home where we had been visiting the leader of the all-girl band that we both had played in earlier in our careers.

They wanted us to get our guitars and come and pick with them. They were called the Foo Fighters and they were going to work at the XCEL Center in St. Paul the next night.

# Foo Fighters pick a core crowd for apple orchard gig in White Bear Lake

By Chris Riemenschneider | SEPTEMBER 14, 2011 — 9:04AM

Dave Grohl at the Foo Fighters' garage show Tuesday in White Bear Lake. / Photos by Doug Nelson, courtesy 93X FM

I asked what they were doing at the apple orchard. It turned out that one of the owner's daughters had won a contest and she could invite fifty of her friends to attend the gathering at the place. The Foo Fighters were going to perform for them in April but there had been a blizzard so they had to reschedule for the September date when they would be in town again. They must have loved the caramel apples though, because they had caramel dripping all over their chins!

We had a nice conversation with some of the guys. As we were leaving a man with a video camera came up and asked if he could interview us. He wanted us to repeat what he had overheard us talking to the band members about. He asked us lots of questions about our music careers and recorded the interview. They sure were pleasant men and we really enjoyed our visit with them.

*Jan Sherman*

# Family

## Lake Owasso Children's Home

My mother, Dorothy, worked at Lake Owasso Children's Home for over 35 years. The Lake Owasso Children's Home was a facility to take care of mentally handicapped young adults. Being the proud mother, she would take Patti's and my recordings to play for the residents at her work. She told us they loved them, and the residents even knew a lot of the lyrics to our songs!

Patti and I loved going there to play a show for them, something we did on many occasions. One time, I asked my sister, Penny, if she would like to come with and help us do the show. I had a little snare drum with a telescoping stand and I showed her how to use brushes to play it and keep time with the music. I thought the residents might enjoy it!

While we were playing, the residents were clapping their hands. They had such great rhythm – it was amazing! Then, the stand that Penny's drum was on, started loosening up. It was slowly collapsing as she played the drum, but it didn't stop her one bit! She just kept on playing it as the drum sank closer and closer to the floor. By the time we finished she was bent over double beating on the drum. The residents thought it was part of the act. Penny didn't miss a beat!

**Jukeboxes**

Patti and I were lucky enough to have our record available on tons of jukeboxes, too. Jukeboxes were big in cafes, bars, and clubs during those years. My oldest son Jeff, who was about four years old at the time, went on a camping trip with his cousin, Dickie, and my parents. They camped out at a site in Big Lake, Minnesota. It started to sprinkle outside, so they left the campsite and drove into town to a small café. Grandpa found the jukebox, deposited his nickels and played a couple of songs. One of them was "Lonely Moonlight," the first song we recorded for MGM. Jeff told the waitress that his mother was the singer on this song. It was obvious to Jeff that she didn't believe him and he became very indignant! "That's my mom and my auntie Pat singing that song!" he insisted. Grandpa explained to the waitress that it was, in fact, his mother singing that song. All of a sudden, Jeff and his grandpa became instant celebrities in the café because of a couple of songs on the jukebox. Many times, the neighbors would come running over to our house yelling, "Your mom is singing on the radio again!" It wasn't a big deal to my sons who weren't too impressed by any of it.

Jonny is the only one of my sons who liked to sing and be on stage. Jeff took piano lessons for a while, but he preferred to be outside. I bought a steel guitar for Jody and he learned how to play one song and that was enough for him. So, when Jonny sang "Ol' Shep" with me at the Como Park Pavilion when he was four years old, I think he got the bug. He picked up playing the guitar quite easily and even took lessons on the harmonica.

## Kelsey Joy

I'm so incredibly proud of my great niece, Kelsey Joy Kopecky, for all she has accomplished in the music industry. What a beautiful young lady she is inside and out. She is a great entertainer with a magnificent voice. She plays every instrument under the sun and tells the most wonderful stories. She is so talented! When she's not entertaining, she's growing vegetables and raising ducks and chickens with her husband on their farm in Nashville. She is multi-talented!

## Family Christmases

Our annual family Christmas parties are so fantastic. Each year, we all gather and marvel at how the nieces and nephews have grown. We're excited to see the new babies that have entered the clan. What a joy it is.

My brother Dan plays guitar and I play the keyboard while everyone sings Christmas carols at the top of their lungs. Santa Claus always manages to find us every year and each child is called to sit on his lap. Then, the kids receive and open their gifts. Some of the hockey-playing nephews will be sitting on the floor holding a cousin's baby and singing all the familiar songs. We are so blessed to have this amazing family to carry on a family tradition like this.

**The Last Chapter**

Now, in my retirement years, I feel so incredibly blessed. I get to spend lots more time with my three wonderful sons and my beautiful grandchildren. How special it is to watch the school activities and sporting events they're involved in. I'm the biggest and loudest cheerleader of them all.

Of course, my longtime love affair with the game of golf keeps me busy. I get to enjoy the beauty of this great land and to spend time with my family and friends. In the winter, I enjoy Arizona. I am also passionate about hunting and fishing. Being the mother of three very active boys, we got to do a lot of that. I still enjoy every chance I get to cast a line or go goose hunting with my eldest son. Such fun! My keyboard gets dusted off once in a while and I play my guitar occasionally too. More recently I started strumming on my ukulele.

My hope is that my grandchildren will remember the times we have shared the joy of music together. Some of them play guitar, ukulele, organ, flute, saxophone, harmonica, drums, and piano. We even had a steel guitar and a steel drum. It makes me so happy to listen to them when they play music for me. They are all so beautiful and talented and are loved more than words could ever tell. Thank you Lord for all of your many blessings!

*Me and my siblings--Patty, Penny, Dan, Jan, & Butch*

Made in USA - Crawfordsville, IN
39488_9798566637853
03.22.2022 1054